COUNTDOWN

TO COLLEGE

THE ESSENTIAL STEPS

TO YOUR CHILD'S

SUCCESSFUL LAUNCH

Monique Rinere, Ph.D.

Praise for COUNTDOWN TO COLLEGE

"This book is a wonderful resource for parents and their children to help them through the critical time from the end of high school through the beginning of college. It provides a thorough guide, keen insights, and practical advice for navigating this important transition."

—Sanjeev R. Kulkarni, dean of the faculty, Princeton University

"Finally, an excellent book about the college-entry process *after* admissions! This book is unique because it recognizes how both students and parents have to understand and confront together every detail of college finances, academics, social life—in short, the college experience as a whole. With remarkable detail, Rinere describes what parents need to do and how prospective students should prepare for college. Her lucid and accessible prose clarifies the process by drawing our attention to issues we might never have considered. Rinere uses powerful anecdotes to explain exactly how carefully we need to plan for our children's futures. In short, she demystifies college for students and parents. This book should be read by every parent of a prospective college student, but it is also especially important for first-generation and disadvantaged families. Beautifully written, incredibly helpful, it will become widely read."

—Karen Barkey, Haas Distinguished Chair of Religious Diversity, professor of sociology, UC Berkeley

"*Countdown to College* is an excellent and practical guide for helping your child choose the best college for them and for getting the most out of the experience once they get there. It gives great advice to parents who want their child to have a successful transition to college life."

—Suzy M. Nelson, Ph.D., vice president and dean for student life, Massachusetts Institute of Technology

"*Countdown to College* is a valuable and comprehensive guide for parents of college-bound students, whether first-timers or veterans. My youngest child started college just as I was reading it, and I found its advice both helpful and calming. The months between high school and college are a critical time, but with this book you can relax (a little) and breathe deeply—Dr. Rinere gives you confidence that everything will be all right."

—Marvin Krislov, president, Pace University

"This is an indispensable guide for college parents—and school counselors—that is by turns reassuring and utterly eye-opening. Dr. Rinere offers essential advice on how a family, working together, can successfully navigate the rocky stretch from 'Congratulations, you're in!' to 'Welcome home for the holidays!' College is intended to be an intellectual and personal adventure; Rinere is there to ensure that it's also an immensely positive one."

—Kerry Walk, president, Marymount Manhattan College

COUNTDOWN TO COLLEGE

COUNTDOWN TO COLLEGE

THE ESSENTIAL STEPS TO YOUR CHILD'S SUCCESSFUL LAUNCH

MONIQUE RINERE, PH.D.

BALLANTINE BOOKS NEW YORK

Countdown to College is a work of nonfiction. With a few exceptions, the people and situations depicted are composites based on the author's experiences.

A Ballantine Books Trade Paperback Original

Published in the United States by Ballantine Books, an imprint of Random House, a division of Penguin Random House LLC, New York.

BALLANTINE and the HOUSE colophon are registered trademarks of Penguin Random House LLC.

LIBRARY OF CONGRESS CATALOGING-IN-PUBLICATION DATA
Names: Rinere, Monique, author.
Title: Countdown to college: the essential steps to your child's successful launch / Monique Rinere.
Description: New York: Ballantine Books, 2019. | Includes bibliographical references and index.
Identifiers: LCCN 2018051126| ISBN 9781524799311 (paperback) | ISBN 9781524799304 (ebook)
Subjects: LCSH: College student orientation—United States—Handbooks, manuals, etc. | Education, Higher—Parent participation—Handbooks, manuals, etc. | BISAC: FAMILY & RELATIONSHIPS / Life Stages / Teenagers. | EDUCATION / Parent Participation. | STUDY AIDS / College Guides.
Classification: LCC LB2343.32 .R56 2019 | DDC 378.1/98—dc23 LC record available at https://lccn.loc.gov/2018051126

Printed in the United States of America on acid-free paper

randomhousebooks.com

987654321

Book design by Diane Hobbing

To Dad, Mom, Lisa, and Toby

CONTENTS

Introduction: The Changes Ahead   xi

Part I: Choosing Wisely   1

Chapter 1: Financial Considerations: What's It Really Going to Cost?   5

The *Real* Net Price of College   7

The Ins and Outs of Work-Study   8

The All-Important EFC   10

When Financial Aid Comes Up Short   12

The Lowdown on the Cost of Studying Abroad   15

Books and Activities Costs Add Up   16

College Breaks Can Be Expensive, Too   16

Factoring In Health Insurance   17

Reading the Fine Print   20

Summer Savings   21

Figuring Out What's Comfortable   22

Chapter 2: Assessing "Fit": From Location to Social Life   26

Revisiting the Academic and Nonacademic Options   31

The Campus Community   52

Food, Glorious Food!   75

What If Your Child Didn't Get In Where They Want
to Go . . . or Wants to Take Some Time Off?   77

Part II: Four Months to Go: Staying Sane from May to August

83

Chapter 3: The Dangers of Slumping Through Spring 85
Pre–Culture Shock 90
Forms and More Forms! Responding to
All Those College Communications 92
The Housing Application and the Importance of Being
Honest 93
Mandatory Summer (and Orientation) Educational
Programs 96
What's the Deal with *Pre*-orientation? 98
Why Colleges Require Orientation 102
Managing Your Own Malaise: Your First Primer
on Self-Care 103

Chapter 4: Summertime Strategies 109
The Formula-for-Life Problem 110
The Pros and Cons of an Independent Major 123
Time to Focus on Your Own Future, Again! 126
A Typical College Week: Structurelessness
and Serendipity 131
It's Your Summer for Change, Too 138

Chapter 5: The Dog Days 144
Make a Communication Plan! 146
The All-Important Health Network 149
The Keys to Packing 156
Seriously, Don't Ignore the Residential Policies Manual 160
The Final Must: Rest, Rest, and More Rest 161
Saying Goodbye, Saying Hello 163
Visualizing Your Life After Drop-off 166

Part III: Starting Strong

169

Chapter 6: September Transitions 171
The Countless Sources of Support 175
What Most Students Miss Out On: Connecting with
Faculty 177
What Do You Still Have to Do with It? 185
It's Your Turn! 194

Chapter 7: Fall Encounters   196
    The Infamous College Partying   199
    A Word or Two About Sex   203
    Why and How to Curb Compulsive Sociability   204
    Finding Their Niche on the Global Stage   207
    Back to You   214

Chapter 8: Finishing Strong   218
    The Initial College Grades   218
    Turning to Your Family and Love Relationships   224
    Home Again   226

Acknowledgments   229

Additional Resources   233

Notes   237

Index   243

INTRODUCTION

The Changes Ahead

As the parent of a high school senior headed to college soon, you've made it through years of preparations for this moment. You have the acceptances and rejections in hand and merely have to send in a deposit to reserve your child's seat in a first-year class. Congratulations! This is a watershed moment in all of your lives.

This book distills what I have learned over years of caring for and advising college students and parents to help you make the college experience as rich as possible for yourself and your child. My goal is to help you be the proud parent of a young adult who stays in college and becomes a degree-wielding alum who is ready to create the next chapter of their lives, just as you engage in a process of creating yours.

As a dean at three Ivy League schools, I have had a front-row seat to the struggles of thousands of new students and their parents. Even at elite, highly selective institutions like Princeton, Harvard, and Columbia, where I worked, people struggle daily. Every new student grapples with making a successful transition to college—to remain healthy, happy, grounded, and in school. And parents suffer, sometimes to an unbearable extent, with letting go and redefining their lives without the child. I cannot count the number of tear-filled conversations I have held with parents who said they found themselves shockingly upset, anxious, depressed, and even inconsolable during this period. It is essential, therefore, not only that you help your children create a conceptual bridge from where they are, a graduating high school senior, to where they want to be, a college alum, but also that you yourself take this as an invigorating opportunity to reinvent your life in new and intentional ways, whether it is your first or last child who is heading off to college.

I've known parents who didn't listen to their child when he told them where he wanted to enroll, furtively lived on their son's floor for two years, or stayed so enmeshed with their college freshman's schoolwork that an academic dean had to warn them that what they did amounted to plagiarism and could result in a one-year suspension of their son. You don't want to be one of those parents. And you don't want your child to be one of these:

- The one in three freshmen who doesn't show up for sophomore year
- The more than 50 percent of students who don't complete a bachelor's degree in six years
- The almost one-half of students who don't get a four-year degree in their lifetime

The United States is experiencing what can only be called a college dropout disaster. There are currently twenty million undergraduates enrolled in college. Out of every hundred students, only thirty-five are reaching the goal we hope for when a student is admitted—that is, they complete the degree and are employed in a position that requires it. Another twenty-eight have graduated but are not in a job that necessitates the degree they just worked so hard to get. And the rest don't have that proverbial sheepskin yet and are more than likely living under a mountain of debt.

I believe this qualifies as a national education crisis. Our success rate is abysmal. We are failing our students and therefore our society and the organizations that humans create to run and enhance our world.

What is going on here? To be brutally honest, I believe that our colleges are not capable of supporting every student who enters them. Their structures are outdated and their funding limited. The academic and nonacademic support scaffolding is staffed by people who are underpaid and overworked. The faculty are pulled in too many directions and are increasingly part-time and also distressingly undercompensated. What's worse, too few of our colleges focus enough on guaranteeing that students accrue the skills and knowledge that are valued and desired in the world of work. So, what is to be done? How do you ensure that your child will cross the stage at graduation?

Parents and children have work to do—together and separately—to rise to the challenges of college and beat the odds against them. The process is not finished when the admission decisions have arrived. On the contrary, a new array of tasks awaits both of you. The stark reality is that many if not most families encounter problems they have not anticipated but could have avoided. Things can go well, but students and their parents need to prepare themselves to avoid the common pitfalls that I have witnessed for decades.

Once you and your children receive responses from colleges, you enter a key period that is divided into three distinct seasons: the decision-making period before you make the deposit (unless you are one of the lucky few whose children were accepted Early Decision or who acted on a positive Early Action response), the summer months before move-in, and the first semester of college. Regardless of whether your child plans to enter a two- or four-year, public or private, small or large college or university, from the moment you anxiously make your way through the offers of admission, you find yourselves meandering through a landscape of unknowns and uncertainties together.

Targeted preparations in these three distinct periods will ensure that you choose well as a family and that your child finishes high school strong and is set up to excel in the all-important first semester. This, in turn, will ensure that a firm foundation for future success is laid and your child ends up on the right side of the graduation statistics. By winter break, you will all be able to celebrate the fruitful establishment of exciting, just as loving, but more independent lives.

This preparation period is even more necessary given that parents are faced with two challenges simultaneously. Since the average U.S. high school student receives only about thirty-eight minutes of college advising from a guidance counselor, you are naturally called upon to deliver the rest. You have no choice but to play a major role in the admission and preparation process. Simultaneously, you are also preparing for a watershed moment in your own life—the absence of your child, who has been the focus of your energy, money, and other resources for a very long time. That means that you, too, have to take a moment to understand what the impending separation will mean for your day-to-day life and overarching self-definition, and plan to make this a win for the whole family.

How do you do that? First things first. Now that you have the acceptances and rejections in hand, you and your rising freshman have to make it through the decision-making process. I know you have already spent hours upon hours thinking about the differences between this school and that one, but now is the time to dive more deeply into the details and discover some of the most essential but often neglected information about the schools you are still considering. Part I invites you to ask one last time: What do they really cost? What do the surrounding areas offer in the way of options for coursework, internships, jobs, and fun? What about the actual academic offerings and support? What is a student's social and residential life like? Once you have the answers to all of those questions and more, you will have the information you need to make the right choice with your child. Even if your choice has already been made via Early Decision or Early Action, this section will help you learn more about your child's future alma mater, which will help them immeasurably as they prepare for move-in and transition to college life.

Part II takes you from your initial deposit through packing and planning goodbyes. First off, your senior may understandably be battling senior slump, a natural reaction to the years-long race to college admission. Meanwhile, you all have to read the mountains of emails and snail mail information and respond to the seemingly endless inquiries that descend upon you from the college. And you, as the parent, will take your first mental steps toward a consideration of your life separate and apart from your child—even if it's just the first of a few children who will eventually head out on their own life adventures—by reflecting on the most important aspects of your well-being.

June and July are the months for helping your rising freshman think about course choices against the background of the "formula-for-life" problem, which is the absence of a surefire recipe for realizing post-college dreams. It will help you understand the lack of a direct correlation between majors and careers so that you can help your rising freshman think about academic and professional choices expansively. At the same time, you will be encouraged to engage in a parallel project, the initial reconsideration of your own professional life against the background of your financial health.

Then, while assisting your soon-to-be college student to construct a realistic fall schedule, taking into account their academic and social obligations (something that is trickier than it sounds), you can take a beat to think about your own social and community life to prepare for the changes ahead.

And finally, August will be the month to really get ready—emotionally and logistically—for drop-off while your freshman is packing, preparing and, hopefully, resting, resting, and resting some more. While asking you to think about what your fall will look like, these chapters prepare you and your rising freshman for the college experience.

Then comes move-in. Part III takes you from drop-off to winter break. You will learn about freshman culture shock, the diversity your child will encounter in all of its many meanings, the ways in which first-semester students face the question of their potential roles on the global stage, how you can help them finish strong, and how best to align your respective expectations for winter break.

As you have already undoubtedly noticed, while you are learning about your child's future challenges, you are also being encouraged to consider your own as a way of preparing you to open yourself up to new things. Not only will it rejuvenate and fortify you, but it will also parallel your child's experience. You will search for and find new things that make life gratifying, productive, and fun, just as your new college student will. This simultaneous and parallel adventure offers you new ways to connect with each other and stay close experientially, even at a geographical distance.

My hope for your child is that his or her college years will be that quintessentially singular time in life that evokes lifelong warm and happy memories. I also hope that this next stage in their lifelong educational journey will lead to a first post-college job and a fulfilling professional life.

Let's get started!

PART I

Choosing Wisely

> When you make the right decision, it doesn't really matter what anyone else thinks.
>
> —Caroline Kennedy

Now that your child has been admitted to three, four, or all of the ten, fifteen, or twenty schools on their list (you would not be alone if this is the number you ended up with), how are they going to decide which offer to accept? Before accepting a spot in the freshman class, there is a whole new set of questions to ask and answers to consider. Sure, since the college application process started, you have been comparing and contrasting one college with another. But now, with the acceptances in hand, a deeper dive will make the final decision as clear and easy as possible. After all, a lot of time has passed since your child began constructing the list of potential schools. Maybe not in terms of the actual number of days that have gone by, but surely in terms of what they have thought about and learned about themselves and the colleges. Students who visit campus on Admitted Students Days always seemed to me years older than the college-touring prospective applicants, as if the process itself had catapulted them into a new level of maturity in record time.

This section leads you through a thoughtful consideration of the most important aspects of each school's offerings, some of which you have probably breezed over in the initial research phase. They fall into two main areas. First and foremost are the financial consider-ations. Unless you can pay full freight, it is imperative that you have all the information you need to avoid falling into the college debt trap, the pernicious result of what Temple University professor of education Sara Goldrick-Rab calls "the new economics of college in America." Then you will launch into the ultimate investigation of the essential college fit: geography and demographics, academic and nonacademic offerings and support, social and residential life, and parental engagement. This will help you avoid the pitfalls that many families fall into. You may say, "But I asked all of these questions in the application process!" Still, your child is changing and the college application process changes people's minds, too. So it's worthwhile to pose these fundamental "fit" questions anew as you assess the op-tions you now know that you have. After all, the most important thing is that the final choice is the best school for your child and your pocketbook.

What If You Did ED/EA and Are Done?

First, congratulations. You have been lucky. Your child chose a school, and the school chose your child. You belong to a small but fortunate minority who have escaped months of work and turmoil.

Second, knowing what the coming years will cost is still important. Chapter 1 will help you figure that out.

Third, Chapter 2 will ensure that you align your expectations and your child's on the academic and nonacademic fronts, so give it a whirl.

CHAPTER 1

Financial Considerations: What's It Really Going to Cost?

Let's face it: Money is always complicated. For college-bound families, it can be the most complex part of the whole equation. About two-thirds of students end up taking out loans to complete college, and the average national debt load per graduate hovers in the tens of thousands. It takes decades to pay the money back, unless students get very well-paying jobs immediately after college and prioritize getting out of debt. Loans made to parents and students will carry different interest rates and require that repayment start at different times. Lenders may or may not require you to start repayment while your child is still in college. Some will offer a six-month grace period after graduation, but interest will begin accruing as soon as you watch them walk across the stage. Most loan programs have a deferment option if you find yourself unable to pay at any given time, but the interest will likely continue to accrue during that period. Parent loans usually require that monthly payments be made toward the principal and interest while the student is still in school.

Why am I going on and on about this? Because many parents and students just sign financial aid forms, loan agreements, and other important documents without reading them! This is a mistake. When I ask a parent or student how much they have borrowed and at what interest rates, they should know the numbers right off the top of their heads. Since most people do not talk about financing college, much less read the fine print, they are unaware of the repayment terms for any of their debts. Let's make sure you go into this with your eyes wide open.

Federal statistics suggest that the overwhelming majority of degree-seeking students receive some sort of aid, whether in the form of grants or loans. About nine of ten first-time degree- or certificate-seeking full-time undergraduate students at four-year institutions receive some sort of financial assistance. In other words, almost no one pays full price. (Likewise, what it costs the institution per student is always far more than the sticker price. The rest is paid by income from state and federal sources, fundraising, and the universities' endowments.)

If you are the parent of one of the 90 percent of students who will receive support of some sort or another, you have already filled out the FAFSA and will continue to do so every year. But the college cost landscape is complex, so the answers to several key questions will interest you. This is not intended to be a comprehensive guide to aid. There are, after all, many books, not to mention not-for-profit and for-profit consultants, solely dedicated to helping you understand the best ways to pay for college. What follows is a quick guide to some of the most important issues you'll face if receiving financial assistance is important to you.

The *Real* Net Price of College

All colleges publish a cost of attendance, also known as the "sticker price." From that number, subtract all aid offered to get the "net price." Since the average student pays only about half of the advertised total cost, you will often hear the advice that you should only pay attention to your net price for any given school because this is the amount it will cost your child to attend this college. In other words, it is the figure you will need to come up with after taking into account the grants and scholarships the school has decided to offer. If a college receives federal funding, and almost every single one does, there must be a net price calculator available on their website to make the calculations as clear as possible. Remember, though, that since your financial situation is unique, your number will be different from those of the other families unless you are all paying full freight.

But you aren't done yet. The actual cost of four years may be much higher, based on course choices (because books and course fees can add up), transportation costs, laundry and dry cleaning habits, groceries above and beyond a meal plan, extracurricular activities, and your child's downtime preferences. If your college student is pre-med, owns a car, travels home frequently, loves to shop for clothing and shoes, does laundry and dry cleaning weekly, buys groceries daily, and enjoys skiing, the final cost is going to be significantly more than for a student who studies literature, doesn't own a car, tends to stay on campus on the weekends, hates to shop, never buys groceries, and only attends cultural events on campus that are discounted or free for students. So you will want to consider the estimated expenses in each of these categories: potential courses of study (books, fees, and travel), transportation to home and work, clothing, food beyond the dining hall, extracurriculars, and leisure-time preferences.

The Ins and Outs of Work-Study

If your child checks the box indicating they would like to be considered for financial aid and if the college ultimately decides to direct some of their funding toward your child's education, then work-study will almost certainly be part of the overall financial aid package. Ultimately, it will be up to your child to find a federal work-study job on campus and earn the amount stated in the award letter. Students are not given positions automatically. Pay particular attention to the amount, divide it by the number of weeks a student will likely work in that term (remember that it will take a few weeks to settle in and find a job), and you will have the amount they need to earn weekly. Work-study pays by the hour, but the amount will vary. It will be no less than the minimum wage but can be significantly higher, depending on the position.

Let's run through an example. Let's say your son's financial aid package includes $1,250 per term of work-study. The semester is fifteen weeks long, but you estimate it will take your son five weeks to acclimate to campus and find a campus job, which would be completely reasonable. So he will work ten weeks in the fall. That means that he has to earn $125 a week. If the position he finds pays $12.50 per hour, then he will have to schedule ten hours of work per week, which, by the way, is pretty doable, so long as he is mindful of this when creating his fall schedule.

A good rule of thumb is for your child not to plan on more than ten to twelve hours of work per week in the first term, if at all possible. Think of it this way: The college adjustment process itself should be counted as one full additional course. Students may be able to find jobs that allow them to increase their hours in the spring, once they are acclimated to their new lives, so that they earn the whole amount granted for the year.

Colleges typically have long lists of work-study positions available. Every department loves these jobs because the federal government bears the overwhelming majority of the costs, so having a few work-study students on staff doesn't have a negative impact on the budget. Some things to be aware of:

- Some work-study positions, like checking IDs at the library or working in the dining hall, are on campus. Others are off campus—at offsite research facilities or stadiums that may be a bus ride away from the main campus. Remember to add travel time and costs to and from the job into the calculations for your child's weekly schedule.
- Many work-study positions are very flexible; others require that students be present at particular times.
- Some supervisors know that students will disappear during finals; others are less accommodating.
- Some will let students work over fall and spring breaks, and others will require it. Still others will not permit students to work during break periods at all.

All of these factors will affect the student's ability to earn the full amount listed in the financial aid package.

When a student has earned the total work-study amount listed in the award letter, that's it. The limit is set by the federal government's calculations, and there is no appeals process. So that job may very well come to an end because the federal subsidy has run out. To keep a student worker beyond that would mean that the employing department would have to pay the whole salary. If an office has a limited budget, as most do, they will not be able to afford the additional cost. So it's important to keep in mind that a student will not be able to earn more than the amount listed on the aid letter unless the office where they work is willing to hire them outside of the federal work-study program.

If you know your child will need more money than the amount designated in the financial award letter, the most important thing is for the student to have knowledgeable and trusted advisors to help figure out the next best step. When sudden expenses arise, the college might have emergency funds, but your child might not qualify; those funds are usually reserved for family tragedies. The likeliest outcome would be for the student to take out a small loan to carry them to the summer, when they could start working full-time. Note that some students work off campus in local coffee shops, restaurants, or retail shops, but I would not recommend this for most freshmen. They really need to focus on adapting to their new home, adjusting to the academic demands, finding their social niche, and staying healthy.

The All-Important EFC

Your child's financial-aid-package award letter likely includes a line item for the Estimated Family Contribution—the EFC. Since this piece of the puzzle is widely misunderstood, let's spend a few minutes on it.

Let's say a college costs $50,000 per year, that the financial aid award letter indicates a grant of $25,000 (some monies from the federal government and some from the institution itself), and an EFC of $10,000. What this means is, first, the school is expecting you to pay that $10,000 in cash. Second, there is still a gap of $15,000. Most families assume that the school will somehow fill in the remaining dollars. But the truth is that the school is expecting you to find that money elsewhere—usually in the form of loans. Some people turn to grandparents and other relatives. Parents often consider a second or third mortgage. Parents and students alike can take out private loans, but many offer notoriously bad repayment terms. If you find yourself in this position, ask yourself: *Is this really the school I want to send my child to?* If so, think carefully about what that is going to mean in terms of your debt and your child's, both while they are in school and then years down the road when you all have to pay the funds back. It may feel like it's too late to turn back. But until you have made the deposit, it is not. This is the perfect time to consider all of the options. Note that even at the very few colleges that boast they meet full need, students end up taking out loans. Take a look at the website for the Project on Student Debt (see the Additional Resources section) for revelatory reports on the national student debt landscape and detailed college-by-college data.

Financial aid offices can be pretty tricky. They are trying to make the college appealing so that you will say yes, but their bottom line is fixed. So you may find that from year to year they increase the "self-help" portion of the aid package. That means that students will need to work more, during the year and in the summer, to "help themselves" to meet the costs of tuition, room, board, and fees. In a case like this, the grant dollars aren't being increased, but the student's responsibility is. It can really feel like a shell game.

The rising number of students who can't afford to eat and house themselves is staggering. Just about every college has hungry, homeless students. Sometimes you hear about a student living in the library or a lounge, tucking their sleeping bag behind some furniture while they are in class. Food pantries are popping up on campuses everywhere, and faculty and administrators are called upon to donate not only basic foodstuffs but personal hygiene products and paper goods as well. In higher-ed parlance, this is called "food and housing insecurity." Faculty are even being encouraged at some schools to add a basic needs statement to their syllabi, like this one from Oregon State University: "Any student who has difficulty affording groceries or accessing sufficient food to eat every day, or who lacks a safe and stable place to live, and believes this may affect their performance in the course, is urged to contact the Human Services Resource Center (HSRC) for support. . . . The HSRC has a food pantry, a textbook lending program, and other resources to help. Furthermore, please notify the professor if you are comfortable in doing so. This will enable them to provide any resources that they may possess." This is truly an alarming and sad state of affairs.

When Financial Aid Comes Up Short

Sonia, one of my all-time favorite students, was one of four children in a single-parent household. Her mother, Alicia, had been disabled for years, so the family scraped by on Social Security, disability, and other forms of federal and state aid. Alicia was, in spite of her circumstances, determined to send her children to college. When Sonia arrived on her campus, she made two false assumptions: (1) that her "full need" package would obviate the need for loans while in college, and (2) that she would not be able to study abroad because of the additional costs she would incur. She was absolutely adamant that she graduate from college without debt. She wanted to get a good job and help her mother as soon as possible, and did not want to be saddled with a large monthly payment to Sallie Mae. The first thing she quickly learned was that the financial aid package did not leave her with any pocket money for occasional expenses in the very tony little college town. On the advice of her advisor, she appealed her financial aid package and was awarded an additional $3,000, thereby avoiding a loan that year.

If you truly want your child to attend a college that has not offered you enough money to make it feasible, the best thing to do *immediately* is to appeal the award. If the college wants you as much as you want them, they will find more funds for you. If the college does not come up with extra funding, you may want to consider another option. Be sure to pay attention to the appeal process and timing. Get the name of a financial aid officer and stay in touch with them. Don't be afraid to ask them for advice on creating the appeal before you submit it. If you end up getting an additional aid award, thank them with a handwritten note or a box of chocolates when you arrive on campus. Financial aid officers do this work because they believe in college access and want to help students fund their education, but there is rarely enough money to go around, so they end up dealing with a lot of testy people on a fairly regular basis. Money never seems to bring out the best in us. It's not surprising that financial aid offices face morale and staff retention issues constantly.

Families often wonder what factors colleges consider when deciding whether or not to grant aid. The most honest answer to this question is: It depends, and it is complicated. For starters, some colleges use the FAFSA, while others depend on the College Board's College Scholarship Service (CSS) Profile. A few even require both. The assets and income considered will vary depending on which form the college uses. And the formulae they rely on change every year depending on enrollment and the ever-rising costs of running a school, along with the unexpected expenses that pop up.

If you cannot find detailed answers to questions regarding the calculations, the best thing to do is to call the financial aid office, learn the name of an officer, and follow up with that person for any further questions. This can be frustratingly difficult, since financial aid officers are typically assisting hundreds if not thousands of families. Keep in mind that it is not unusual for a college with a higher sticker price to end up costing less than a school that boasts a lower price. Do not make any assumptions about the final cost without doing research and the math.

One unpleasant question you may want to ask is what the college does if the family circumstances change suddenly in the coming years. Often the aid package cannot be changed quickly or at all to accommodate that. If a parent loses a job, for example, the college may not be able to respond favorably to a need for greater aid. Incoming students and their parents never think to ask this question, because, well, who plans on tragedies? But the answer can be surprising, so it may pay to ask. Because if the college says "probably not" or "not right away," it will be up to you to take out more loans or your child may have to take a leave of absence. I have seen many, many students forced to take time off from school because their aid package was not adjustable to reflect a parent's sudden illness, loss of employment, or a family tragedy. These are truly heartbreaking situations.

If your child does not apply for aid as an incoming student, it is possible that it won't be something they can do in the future. I once knew a student from China named Jane whose parents never imagined finding themselves in a precarious financial situation, so they never thought to apply for aid during the application process. When the family lost everything in a precipitous economic downturn, Jane turned to her college's financial aid office, only to learn to her dismay and disbelief that she was ineligible for aid because she had not applied initially. The school funded few international students, and all of the awards had already been granted. Jane took a two-year leave of absence to earn the money she needed to finish her degree.

Unless you are 100 percent certain that you will never need it, you ought to apply as soon as possible and reapply every year. This ensures that you will be able to legitimately inquire about extra funding if your family faces unexpected misfortunes. It will not guarantee that you will receive additional aid, but at least you will be in the running. Colleges want admitted students to graduate so that they can include them in the nationally reported (and highly scrutinized) graduation rates. Remember the national graduation statistic? Only about half of students complete a degree in *six* years. That means they have taken multiple semesters off. It is so important to the college that your child finishes the degree at their institution that there may be wiggle room if circumstances change. You may have to ask more than once, and be prepared to elevate your request higher and higher up the ranks of the university administration.

One more note about financial aid: What they don't tell you about outside aid may stun you. Let's say your child has received a financial aid package from a number of schools, and the college at the top of the list leaves your family with a gap of $5,000 (the difference between the cost and your EFC plus aid). Your very industrious kid decides to apply for some of the scholarships listed in one of those catalogs chock-full of thousands of sources of external aid, and is granted $5,000 from your local Rotary Club. You think you are done.

College is paid for. But wait! Once the college receives the external funds, it may very well reduce your child's financial aid package by that exact amount. In other words, they might *subtract* $5,000 from your child's financial aid award because they have not changed their minds at all about the amount your family should pay and the gap you have to meet. They will see the outside grant as a benefit in that it reduces the institutional cost of supporting your child. I hasten to add that if the college reduces the aid package because of the outside monies, it may still be a good idea to pursue aid from external sources, since grants often carry prestige. Having that appear on a résumé cannot hurt. But the external aid may not help achieve your initial goal of reducing the gap.

The Lowdown on the Cost of Studying Abroad

At many colleges, the basic cost to study abroad or away is the same as studying on the home campus. And in most cases, if the destination is less expensive than the home institution, you will be charged the regular tuition. Of course, local expenses might be lower, so less pocket money will be needed, but you will probably not save on tuition or other college fees. Another thing to keep in mind is that you may not receive help with travel costs to and from the campus abroad.

Remember Sonia? Her second false assumption was that she would not be able to afford a semester abroad. During an initial conversation, her advisor asked her if she was planning to study in another country while in college, and Sonia said sheepishly that she could not afford it. She was amazed to learn that studying abroad would cost the same as studying on campus, and that, in fact, the aid package would follow her abroad. Plus, the college had an application process to access grant funds for travel. She happily went to Spain for her sophomore spring, where she met her future husband!

Books and Activities Costs Add Up

Some of this has been mentioned already, but it is probably worth emphasizing that the net price of a college education will increase as other fees accumulate over time. Courses often carry high fees. Books and lab fees can be astronomically expensive. The average science major pays thousands more for chemistry and biology books than their English-major peers spend on novels. Music lessons, club sports, certifications, travel for extracurriculars—it all adds up. You may want to ask current parents on Facebook or College Confidential if you cannot find the costs of your child's anticipated activities on the school's website. Such costs add up quickly, and if your student is truly interested in pursuing expensive activities, they may have to work more or take out bigger loans than originally planned.

College Breaks Can Be Expensive, Too

As part of the overall college cost calculation, many colleges include only one trip home per year. Then, if a student cannot afford to travel home for fall, winter, or spring break, the cost of housing and meals for those weeks is probably not built into the package. Some dormitories close completely during breaks, so students have to find alternative places to stay, which can also be expensive. Some dorms stay open but dining halls close, so students have to buy groceries or go to restaurants. I have known students who could not afford to spend any money on food and relied exclusively on their dining plans, so they spent the break week hungry or trying to find friends in the area who would invite them home. This is a miserable way to spend time off from classes when they are supposed to be resting, eating well, and storing up energy for the weeks to come. If the costs of housing, meals, and travel are of concern to you, be sure to ask what the policies are at your child's potential schools.

Factoring In Health Insurance

Another source of great confusion for students and parents is the college's policies on health insurance. If your child has an ongoing medical issue, this is obviously particularly important. But even if they don't, you never know what a young person is going to need in the coming years with respect to physical and mental healthcare. Being aware of the ins and outs of the availability and costs can save you a great deal of money, time, and frustration.

Ask what level of health insurance, if any, has been calculated into the cost of attendance. Find out if there are other options and, if so, what they will cost. If you plan to keep your child on your insurance, look up the college's policies regarding parental insurance. You may be required to fill out a waiver, and the college may or may not approve your application if your insurance is not considered adequate in the college's state. If your insurance is approved, find out if your child will still be able to access the college's medical facilities, and if so, which ones. Their access to these may be restricted in some ways. Pay close attention to the college's health insurance recommendations. They are established based on years of experience with kids just like yours.

If your son or daughter suddenly falls ill, these questions become really important. In the scrum of a crisis, finding the answers can be extremely aggravating. Most health crises on college campuses take place at night or on the weekends, when, of course, the insurance office is closed. Even the on-call team that responds to crises will not know the answers to your insurance coverage questions. Why would they? Even if they say they do, their knowledge will be restricted to particular situations they have experienced in the past, not necessarily yours.

A student named Kaitlyn was waiting to get to college to have a tumor on her pituitary gland treated. She and her parents assumed the college insurance would cover whatever she needed, so the family did not pay much attention to the health insurance options that were described in one of the seemingly hundreds of brochures they received over the summer. When Kaitlyn went to the health services office, she learned that not only could they not treat her there, but the outside specialists she needed were not covered by the insurance she'd picked. If she or her parents had asked questions ahead of time, they would have opted for the higher level of insurance coverage, which would have eased the financial burden the first year imposed on them.

Students with known medical conditions need to take the time beforehand to investigate all of their insurance and treatment options. I cannot stress this enough. There is nothing to fear; the college will not revoke their acceptance. In fact, if they did, they would be violating the Americans with Disabilities Act, which every college takes very seriously, as they should. If you let the staff know about conditions ahead of time, then you can work together to put the best treatment plan in place well in advance of your child's arrival.

Even if your child doesn't have a medical condition, it is worthwhile to learn everything you can about the insurance cost and coverage options as well as the university's health services offerings. Hopefully, you will never need to lean on them, but if you do, you will be glad you informed yourself in advance.

Additionally, if your child hopes to study abroad (which, frankly, I recommend to virtually every student), you should find out what health insurance options are available during the time in a foreign country. If they fall ill while there, does the insurance cover medical evacuation (medevac) to your home hospital of choice or to the hospital of the insurance's choice? Or will your family's insurance cover it? Does the college work with International SOS or a company like it that provides international medical assistance and emergency and evacuation services? This sort of provider is essential in case your child falls ill or winds up in the midst of a natural or human-made disaster of some sort, such as an earthquake or an act of terrorism. This is not meant to scare you, but rather to help you prepare for the unforeseen.

Many schools will require that your child have supplemental insurance while abroad that will cover things like medevac costs, but the insurance company may only cough up the funds if it deems the charges "medically necessary." That means that they may not cover transportation to your home hospital if the medical services can be rendered abroad. Having your kid hospitalized in a foreign country, without family, without your own trusted physician, and possibly being treated by medical staff who speak a foreign language that your child may not have fully mastered yet is not a desirable situation for anyone. Again, most families will not need to know the answers to these questions, but if you are one of the few who will, you will be grateful you took the time to research your child's coverage ahead of time.

Consider the example of Kayla, a first-generation student who had won a distinguished fellowship to study literature in her mother's home country, Tunisia. She was beyond excited. On her first sightseeing trip, her bus slipped off a steep embankment and rolled over several times. When she woke up, she was in an ambulance speeding toward a hospital. Within a few hours, she was released. But for days later, she felt a nagging pain in her back, so she went to another doctor and learned that her back was fractured in several places and needed immediate care, which was not available at that facility. She contacted the fellowship director, who said that he could not help her. When she looked into the insurance coverage, she discovered they would only transport her to Europe. Her family did not have the funds to medevac her home, so Kayla decided to be moved to Frankfurt, Germany, where she could not only get good care but be assisted by a college friend's family who lived nearby. She spent a year there convalescing and had to take a year off before resuming her studies.

If Kayla and her family had looked into the fellowship's insurance policies and paid particular attention to the restrictions, they could have invested a small amount of money in an international health insurance policy that would have covered the cost of moving Kayla to her home city.

Reading the Fine Print

You may be thrilled to receive a great deal of aid the first year only to discover that the college has frontloaded the funds that don't have to be paid back. They may very well load you up with loans in subsequent years, which will mean that all of your initial calculations will be off. In other words, students are not necessarily guaranteed a stable or equivalent financial package from year to year even though the costs will rise annually at the vast majority of institutions. By now, you should have the name of one or two financial aid officers, so if you don't know if this will be the case for your child and can't find guidance on the college's website (which would not be surprising), then call the office and ask. If they are less than forthcoming, be persistent until you have your answer. Before you commit to a college, you need to know what your and your child's total debt will be upon graduation, assuming that your family's financial situation does not change. At this point, the best you can do is to make your calculations based on what you know and be aware of the options if the unexpected happens.

Be sure to ask about the limits and conditions for continued aid. Here are some questions to start off the conversation:

- Does financial aid remain relatively consistent from year to year with respect to the proportion of grants and loans in your package?
- How does the school accommodate the annual increases in tuition and other fees?
- Will aid end after a certain number of semesters, regardless of whether the student has completed the degree? (Most colleges cap funding at eight semesters in spite of the fact that half of U.S. students take more than four years to finish.) In other words, how many years of aid is your child eligible for?
- If more than four years is needed, what options are there?

- What happens if a student takes a leave at some point? Early in the semester? Later in the semester? (It does make a difference in terms of refunds and what will end up on the transcript.)
- Are there strings attached to any of the aid?
- Is there a grade point average (GPA) requirement to maintain the aid?
- If your child is a recruited athlete, what happens if they are injured and can no longer play or simply decide not to?
- What is the average debt load of a graduating senior? (Be sure to check out the website for the Project on Student Debt.)

Summer Savings

If a financial aid package lists "student summer earnings," your child is expected to work this summer to earn those dollars to dedicate to their education. That is considered part of the family contribution. If they do not earn that amount, you or they are going to have to find another way to pay that amount. If they earn more, the aid will not decrease. Every year, there is a stated maximum amount students can earn without it affecting their aid when applying for funding.

Let's say that your daughter must earn $2,400 this summer. She does so without a problem, working in the same job she has held for the past two years at the local library. But next summer she wants to study abroad. What happens to the student contribution for the following academic year? Some colleges have competitive scholarships to cover summer earnings of financial aid recipients. Keep in mind that the applications are usually due much earlier than you would think, so urge your kid to pay attention to the deadlines. The funding is probably pretty limited, so a loan may be the only option to cover those funds that would have been earned, even if the summer program is college-sponsored.

This is an opportune moment to say something about summer

jobs. High school students may hate the idea, especially given their level of exhaustion. They may just want to relax with their friends and play video games. But working the summer before freshman year has an advantage other than the obvious accrual of some fall spending money. It is getting rarer and rarer for U.S. teenagers to work. Only about a third do it, and the trend is downward. This is, however, a missed opportunity. If your child has held a job for a number of months before college, it sends a distinct and positive signal to all future employers that they won't have to teach them some of the basics of being an employee, like promptness, reliability, acceptable workplace behavior, expected attire, levels of formality versus informality, paycheck taxes, and so on. This is especially important now, when millennials are widely derided for being lazy, unfocused, and impossible to manage in the workplace. Future potential employers look much more favorably upon the résumé of a young person who took the unglamorous summertime position as a lifeguard or fast-food worker than they will on that of an applicant who has never worked before. It signals not only that they proved themselves reliable but also that they have already garnered at least some idea of what the world of work expects of employees. That means less basic training for the future supervisor.

Having a summer job also gives your child some structure to the months before college move-in. Rather than landing in a yawning three-month period of nothingness, the rising freshman faces weeks that already have a shape, which is helpful for most teenagers.

Figuring Out What's Comfortable

It stands to reason that one of the biggest reasons that students do not complete a four-year degree is that they haven't planned well for the cost. Families buckle under the strain, knowing that the discomfort will last for years beyond college. For the majority of families, it is essential to work collaboratively and with a calm head to choose a college that will offer the student and the family the most financial comfort. Statistics show that most students finish college these days with a debt of between $30,000 and $40,000, and that number is increasing rapidly over time. The amount you will have to pay back on a monthly basis will depend on the interest rate and the number of years you are granted to pay back the loan in full. It's time to find a loan calculator and play around with some numbers.

Let's say that your child leaves college with $27,000 in debt at 3 percent interest, with a repayment period of 15 years or 180 months. Using a student debt calculator, you will discover that they will pay more than $6,000 in interest over the 15 years, for a total of over $33,000. What's also important to note is that the loan calculator reveals the minimum salary needed to meet the monthly loan repayment requirement. In this case, a new college graduate would have to earn a total of $26,905.20, with 10 percent of the annual income going to the loan repayment. Whether or not this will be manageable depends, of course, on the cost of living where they end up working.

Let's say the debt is $100,000 at 6.8 percent. Then the monthly hit is going to be $1,151 and the salary would have to be at least $80,000 a year. Given that the average starting salary of new college grads hovers around $50,000, this might be a painful start to post-college life.

If your child has some idea of what they might want to study, you can look up the average salary for college graduates with those majors to see if she will be on track to meet her financial obligations after school. The Hamilton Project, an economic policy initiative of the Brookings Institution, provides a particularly useful tool for researching the range of potential earnings for each of eighty majors. Throughout my career, I have been committed to the idea that students should "pursue their passions," but I now find that it has become a worn-out, uninspiring drumbeat that is out of step with reality. Of course, we should all pursue many of our passions throughout our lifetime, but there is nothing wrong with making decisions with our eyes wide open. You can help your child become aware of the economic reality of their choices.

Where does all of this leave you? Let me share the story of one of my favorite college dads of all time (other than my own, of course): Alexandre. I knew him for just a few minutes, but his clear-eyed calculations and wise communication with his son left a lasting impression on me.

Alexandre had made a good living in Big Pharma after finishing his fully subsidized, no-cost degrees in Europe. He immigrated to North Carolina, married, and had a son, Robert, who excelled in all things science- and math-related. When they started to shop around for a college, Alexandre and Robert looked up the cost of in-state tuition and fees for four years and compared it to the price of attending a private university where they hoped he would gain admission. At that time, the University of North Carolina at Chapel Hill cost about $7,500 a year in tuition (the costs are still admirably low). They calculated another $15,000 for the rest of the college-related expenses, for a total of $90,000 over four years. Alexandre told Robert he could have that amount of money for his undergraduate degree. Where he decided to attend would be completely up to him, as would any expenses beyond that number. The private universities would cost approximately $325,000, so Robert would have to finance more than $235,000 himself.

Though I have worked at several Ivy League schools, and, in fact, was advising students and their parents at one of them when I met Alexandre, I have never thought that going into lots of debt to attend a highly selective school was a great idea. In this case, the choice was clear. Robert prudently chose to attend a state university, finished college with no loans, enjoyed a world-class education, and is happily pursuing a productive career in a community where he already has deep roots and which he loves.

Final Calculations

- How much can you comfortably pay per year for your child's four-year education?
- How much debt do you and your child want to incur? How long will it take you and them to pay it back?
- Given your child's potential major and career interests, will they likely earn enough to pay back the loans?

CHAPTER 2

Assessing "Fit": From Location to Social Life

When people look for a home, they immediately think about the ubiquitous real estate saying: location, location, location. No doubt location played a major role when your child applied to colleges in the first place. Indeed, one of the things most college counselors ask students at the beginning is where they want to be: *What kind of weather do you like/are you used to? How far away from home are you comfortable being? How big a college/university and town/city do you think you want to be in?* The answers to these questions likely helped your child form an application list in the first place. And this might mean that your child limited their possible choices to a certain region, distance from home, or college size. That's half the battle!

But now they're in and you have to drill deeper because (1) your child's feeling about what they are comfortable with may have changed since applying and (2) their happiness over the next four years could depend on knowing more about their new "hometown."

Not only do you have to try to help your child understand what it *really* will be like to live there, but the flavor and makeup of a place will have an impact on the all-important internship and work opportunities for the student while there. That means that the location becomes an important factor in laying the groundwork for future careers.

Why? Because when a student wants to secure volunteer positions, community-based research opportunities, and the increasingly indispensable internships in their potential industries of interest, the offerings in the immediate vicinity of the college become crucial. They also play a determining role in coursework, leisure-time options, and medical care facilities. Plus, the general disposition of the town/city toward the annual presence of hundreds if not thousands of nine-month inhabitants can make the difference between being welcomed and not.

Regardless of whether they are in the countryside, a town, or a city, the institutions your child may attend have a history all their own and surely offer some interesting features that translate into options for students' educational pathways. Some things you will want to research include the demographics of the area; ethnic, religious, and socioeconomic diversity; political leanings and representation; the economy and major businesses; cultural offerings; and indications of the town-gown relationship, that is, the way the college and the surrounding area get along. As you do, you will learn the salient history of the college and area, the number of employees the college employs, the prominent industries, the main challenges of the community, and the numbers and types of schools the university contains and their respective locations.

This does not have to take a lot of time. Just do a quick Wikipedia search on the town and the university, and you'll have more information than you need. Here are some facts to keep in mind:

- The larger a university, the more job options students have and the larger the network of alumni.

- The more local students a university enrolls, the more lifelong connections your child will end up making in that geographical area, perhaps tying them there long after college.
- The more international a student population and the more global the education, the more friends they will be able to visit in other parts of the world both in and after college.
- The demographics of the area translate into real opportunities for college students not only to get to know people who can enrich their lives and have interesting stories to tell but also to engage in community work, service learning, internships, and research, and to land jobs.
- The cultural institutions and major industries in the area most likely hire students as interns and alumni as employees.
- Poverty-stricken areas will offer students untold community service and engagement options, but there may well be tension between the town and the college.
- Overwhelmingly wealthy college towns may have few low-cost leisure-time options and may introduce social discomfort for students from underresourced backgrounds.
- Small college towns will inevitably offer fewer and smaller religious communities.
- The political leanings of the area draw students and, importantly, faculty who hold those beliefs (though many colleges in more conservative regions of the country form small islands of more left-leaning thinking).

This exercise can also be useful for people whose children are going to college near their own home. Even if you have raised your family in a suburb of Boston and your kid is going to attend one of the area's three dozen or so schools only several miles away or your family home is on Long Island and your son is off to Adelphi, do yourself a favor and look at the colleges and the surrounding areas with fresh eyes.

As a parent who will likely visit the campus at drop-off, on Parents' Weekend, and again at graduation (and perhaps several times in between), you will also want to take a look at the hotels, restaurants, shopping, and cultural offerings, all of which become especially important if your child doesn't seem to have a lot of time for you when you visit. Sometimes the lodging options are quite limited (and not so great). In smaller college towns, it is not unusual for parents to have to make hotel reservations years in advance for graduation festivities. Some, like Palo Alto, gouge parents at commencement with hotel rooms that cost many, many hundreds of dollars per night more than usual. Short-term vacation rentals might be a cheaper and more comfortable option.

Sightseeing in the Campus Area

Make a running list of the interesting sights to see and things to do in the areas surrounding your child's potential colleges. Add to them as you hear from other parents through social media or in conversation while visiting. You will be happy to have this list of things to do either with your child or when you are visiting and they are busy.

Katie grew up in Asheville, North Carolina, and knew it like the back of her hand. She had wandered these streets with her parents and friends since she was born. She loved it, but felt deep down that she needed to get away from everything familiar and discover a new place on her own. The location of a college was one of the decisive factors in making her choice. She was open to a small city or a suburb but was not crazy about the idea of large cities or farming communities. She had not applied to any schools in Boston, for example, because she thought it would be too overwhelming. She had also not applied to colleges like Kenyon or Oberlin because the towns were just too small for her. St. Paul, Minnesota, where Macalester is located, seemed perfect to her. She had done a little research and learned that the city had about 300,000 residents, which, while several times larger than Asheville, still seemed completely manageable to her. It had the additional attraction of its twin city, Minneapolis, which was larger and offered a good number of opportunities. Museums, concerts, clubs—the Twin Cities had it all. But St. Paul felt like a smaller, somewhat less intimidating place than Boston or New York City, for example. At this point, she poked around some more, discovered the top ten things to do there, read about the museums and restaurants, and was intrigued by the cities' histories and diversity. The more she learned, the better she felt about this as her college home.

April Research

Look up the following information about the remaining colleges on the list:

- How big is the town geographically?
- How many people live there?
- What are the top ten things to do there? (Check TripAdvisor, for example.)
- What are the names of the museums and galleries?
- What and where are the best and worst restaurants?
- What is the demographic makeup of the place?
- Is there public transportation? Or do you need a car when you visit?
- What is the area famous for historically? Are there monuments or memorials?
- What are the largest employers there? Pharmaceutical companies? Farms? Insurance companies? Factories? Media

firms? (Remember, local employers often hire many students in the summer and during the semester.)

- Are there local sports teams?
- Are there movie theaters? How far are they from the college?
- What is the local government? Is it Republican or Democratic or independent?
- What are the main religions? Are there places of worship of interest on campus or off?
- What is the relationship like between the locals and the college? What are the sources of tension?

These are all obviously factors you have considered in your life when deciding where to live, work, and raise your family. Likewise, they are important considerations now when helping your child choose a college.

Revisiting the Academic and Nonacademic Options

Your high school senior has probably undergone exponential growth in the past few months, and they may now be thinking differently about what they want to study and do in college. With your child changing rapidly, it is worthwhile to make double and triple sure that their ever-evolving expectations and interests align with what the college has on offer. Most families also make assumptions about available academic scaffolding that are perfectly reasonable but equally wrong, especially with respect to things like tutoring, disability services, and faculty availability. As you can imagine, the disappointment in each of these cases is crushing. Because once they have moved in, you have paid, everyone has bought swag, and your child already sees himself or herself as a future alum, there is no turning back! Now—in the assessment-of-fit process—is the time to be sure no one *wants* to turn back down the road.

The Majors, Minors, Centers, and Institutes

If I had a dollar for every time an incoming first-year student responded to my question "What do you want to study?" with the name of a major that does not exist at the schools where I worked, I would have a tidy sum. Scores of students arrive wanting to major in business at a college that does not offer it. Others are interested in linguistics or nanotechnology only to find out that neither is available. Or they want to minor in painting or sculpture even though that has never been a possibility for undergraduates on that campus. Still more plan to take courses at an affiliated law or medical school only to discover too late that these professional schools do not exist there or that cross-registration is next to impossible.

All you have to do to avoid this is to revisit the list of majors and minors. Any college website should have a handy list of them, and the departmental pages will inevitably include a brief description of the field and opportunities for undergraduates. No one should be embarrassed for not knowing what some or even most of them are. The majority of high schools don't offer things like anthropology and sociology, and different colleges can define them very differently. So being able to define what each field means is rare for people who don't spend their lives in higher education.

As you already know, some colleges have some graduate schools and others don't. If your child aspires to take graduate-level courses, what you want to know is which colleges permit undergraduate students to take those courses and how hard it is to cross-register. It might not be permitted. Or it might be possible technically but virtually impossible for other reasons.

In addition to departments and graduate schools, most colleges and universities have affiliated research institutes and centers, which also give undergraduates chances to engage in coursework, internships, and jobs. A quick glance at the college website will reveal these. And a word to the wise: Don't assume that only large universities have these outside opportunities. The two thousand students at Trinity College in Hartford, Connecticut, can enjoy all kinds of opportunities at over a dozen institutes. Even though Siena College has only about three thousand undergraduates, it boasts twenty affiliated institutes. Whether at a small college or a massive state university, work-study jobs and research positions at these centers of academic activity translate into extraordinary learning opportunities and close contact with potentially fascinating faculty. They can also lead to graduate school and jobs.

Speaking of Faculty

Study after study reveals what we know intuitively—that meaningful faculty contact enhances the undergraduate experience. Why? Because professors are the mentors, the classic guides through the academic world. Students should think of faculty as the Merlin of Arthurian legends, as Professor Dumbledore of the Harry Potter series, and as Yoda and Obi-Wan Kenobi from *Star Wars*. They know stuff, and they have made a conscious, deliberate, and often tough decision to devote their lives to teaching, writing, and speaking about a field in which your child may spend at least a third of their college career.

Unfortunately, many students ignore faculty or try to avoid them. This is a big mistake. My most adamant advice to undergraduates is to plan to get to know the faculty. If they do nothing else outside of schoolwork, they ought to do that. How do you find out how possible that will be?

All colleges list the faculty–student ratio. Some even brag about theirs. But these numbers are like all other statistics—that is, subject to interpretation and fiddling behind the scenes. Colleges use the student–faculty ratio as shorthand for how much faculty attention a student should expect to get at that school. If the ratio is 20:1, they reason, a student can anticipate getting less than if the ratio is 7:1. But is that a fair conclusion to draw from those numbers? What more should you find out in order to figure it out?

One of the most important facts will be the number of classes your child will enroll in during freshman and sophomore year that have fewer than twenty-five students. Second is how many of them will likely be taught by full-time tenure-track or tenured professors as opposed to part-time faculty and graduate students. These numbers are way more important than the faculty–student ratio advertised in the campus brochure.

But the answers to these questions are often difficult to find. The antidote to this is to ask current students (who are not on the admission office payroll) during your visits or through online forums. If they seem reticent or coy, I would press them on it because the responses will be revealing. In the first two years, your child will be in search of a major, possibly a minor, and, above all, meaningful academic experiences. These are hard to come by when they find themselves in cavernous halls listening to someone lecturing to hundreds of students at a time. Sure, there are "recitations" or "discussion sections" or some other small-format classroom engagement as part of the course, but these are almost always taught by graduate students or part-time faculty (aka adjuncts). Most undergraduates do not get close to a full-time faculty member until junior year. Even the "freshman seminars" that have been designed to fix this problem are frequently taught by graduate students and part-timers. I am not suggesting that they aren't valuable teachers. In fact, many of them are superb. But they may not be around for four years, and their priorities are not your children. Graduate students are trying to complete a degree, and adjuncts are mostly focused on cobbling together a life with a series of horribly undercompensated positions. Tenure-track or tenured faculty are more committed to the institution, are more established in their fields, and are in it for the long haul. When it comes time to write a junior paper or senior thesis or to get guidance on some other capstone project, your child will want to work with someone who has taught them in the past. When they look back and see only graduate students and adjuncts, most of whom have moved on, it can be daunting.

Smaller class sizes in the first two years will also translate into more opportunities to speak in class early on and exchange ideas, more detailed feedback on work before they enter the major, more frequent faculty interaction so they can choose advisors well, increased confidence, and a closer-knit academic community.

Faculty, Faculty, Faculty

With your child, you should consider all the potential areas of study. Looking at the webpage for each major, consider:

- How many full-time faculty members are there at the institution and in each department of interest?
- Is it easy to find the number of part-timers or adjuncts teaching there? How does that number compare to the number of full-time faculty?
- What is the number of graduate students overall and in each relevant department? (If there are many, know that the faculty will spend a majority of their time with them rather than undergraduates because graduate students are the professors of tomorrow. And the graduate students will be doing a lot of the teaching because that is how they support themselves.)
- What is the number of undergrads majoring in each field your child may pursue?
- Look up the sizes of introductory classes and opportunities for faculty contact. How available and accessible are they? Do they have office hours listed for the course or in gen-

eral? Are there any intro courses that have fewer than twenty to twenty-five students in the first two years?

- What do current students have to say about faculty interaction? You may be able to get some of the answers only if you talk to current students. Some departments list peer advisors on their webpage, which is a sure sign that the recruitment and guidance of undergraduates is a priority for that department. Be sure to find out how many small-size courses are available in your child's initial four semesters.

- If you can't find the numbers of peer advisors on the website, call the departmental administrator and see if that person will share the information with you.

- If your child has highly developed academic interests, see if the administrator will help your child schedule a time to talk with a faculty member, and see what they say about faculty availability and opportunities for undergraduates.

- Check out the departmental websites for academic community-building initiatives such as a journal, conferences, and other gatherings and events that include faculty, graduate students, and undergrads.

- Search the student newspaper(s) for articles on the departments.

- Ask if students get to evaluate their professors and course experiences regularly, and if so, where the results are publicized.

It may not be easy to get the answers to these questions, even on campus visits. But whatever you are able to find out, know that you are already ahead of the game since most students arrive on campus not knowing any of this.

Some students are happiest in a large department where they have a vast array of academic possibilities. Some enjoy them, however, because they want to avoid faculty and remain relatively anonymous academically. That's a very different college experience from the one a student will have in a small department where they get to know most of the tenured and tenure-track faculty, graduate students, and other undergraduate majors and are welcomed at social and scholarly events.

As you discover the reality behind the numbers, you will realize that colleges generate marketing and public relations campaigns just like any other industry. It's a handy reminder not to let yourself be taken in by the advertised numbers. There is always more to the story. Even if you have no clue what your child will major in, when you work together to learn what you can about the top five to ten subjects on their list, you will paint a much more accurate picture of the place. In the final analysis, I believe that you can have a superlative academic experience on a large state university campus, at a small private college, or at something in between. All it takes is one faculty member to make the difference, but students need contact with them early on and frequently to make that a reality.

Understanding the Study-Abroad Opportunities

Global experiences are essential to a well-rounded education. As I already mentioned, if it were up to me, studying away, as some call it, would be a degree requirement at every institution of higher learning in our country. The sign of its value to students in becoming well-rounded individuals and to their future employers is signaled by the fact that just about every college in the United States now offers its undergraduates opportunities to study (and earn credits toward the degree), do internships, and/or engage in service projects in other countries or in other areas of the United States. Indeed, I subscribe to the tenet best expressed by the president of the Institute for International Education, Allan E. Goodman: "International experience is one of the most important components of a twenty-first-century education, and study abroad should be viewed as an essential element of a college degree. Learning how to study and work with people from other countries and cultures also prepares future leaders to contribute to making the world a less dangerous place." In another article, he and international career expert Stacie Nevadomski Berdan wrote: "Despite the inevitable increasing global competition for jobs, American graduates lack the international experience, language capabilities and cross-cultural communication skills necessary to succeed in the global economy. With only about 10 percent of students studying abroad at some point in their academic career, we have a long way to go." Not only does studying abroad make graduates more marketable professionally, but it also, and more importantly, enables them to grow as people. They become more resourceful, self-confident, and worldly, and learn how to interact productively with those who are very different from them.

Getting to the Details of Study Abroad

With the list of potential schools before you, take a look at the colleges' global programs site, and see if you can find the answers to the following:

- Are undergrads expected to study abroad or away from the campus at some point during their time there?
- What percentage of undergraduates engages in study abroad or other global opportunities?
- When do students normally go, and what are the most popular options?
- How many study-away opportunities are offered?

- How many are sponsored by this college, and how many are approved but sponsored by other colleges?
- Do the departments of interest list any global programs on their webpages?
- Does the college send its own faculty to teach in any of the programs?
- Let's say your child wants to study abroad in a country where English is not the first language. How many semesters of the language do they have to complete before getting on the plane? Or can they begin the language there? If they don't have to know the language when they get there, who will help them navigate the new place? Are there people on the ground who can help with doctor's appointments, visas, cultural practices, and so forth?
- Will the courses and grades appear on the college's transcript? Or will transcripts have to be requested from the sponsoring institution every time they are needed?
- Will the grades they earn abroad figure into the overall GPA?
- Who helps students plan their study-abroad experience? Are there specific advisors for global opportunities?
- How does the school prepare students to go abroad? What sorts of workshops or training are available?
- When they return, is there a dedicated program to help them reflect on what they have experienced and learned while abroad?

Gauging Academic Advising and Support

Academic advising systems, programs, and support differ wildly from one campus to the next. Some colleges invest little or no resources into guiding undergraduates. Others boast that "only faculty advise," which is less something to tout than you might think. Still others have "professional advisors" in addition to or instead of faculty advisors. Before you reach your final decision, take a few minutes to understand what resources will be available on an ongoing basis to help your child with the many decisions that will inevitably have to be faced in the college years.

College and high school advising differ from each other. Guidance counselors help students complete their high school degree and get into college. A good guidance counselor is worth their weight in gold. They have the patience of a saint and absorb an unbelievable amount of ever-changing information to do their jobs well. They generally handle caseloads that far exceed a reasonable number. If your child's high school guidance counselors were helpful, perhaps try to find a moment to let them know. It will mean a great deal to them—the number of students and parents who thank them is never high enough.

College advisors are something else altogether. They serve as sounding boards to help students make decisions for which there are no formulae. Each advisee is a unique individual who is forging an equally singular path through life. The next step after college is probably unknown at this point. That means that your child will need people who can help them find the best ways to explore their new home and take steps to create their imagined futures.

The more knowledgeable the advisors are, the more they can help each student make decisions to complete the degree on time and prepare to take the right next steps for them once the diploma is in hand. It may seem strange to parents, but not every faculty advisor is knowledgeable about the curriculum, rules, processes, or strategies to finish on time. Even worse, few have the luxury of adequate time to spend with undergraduates since they are being pulled in many directions. (And what's also true is that some really, really don't like spending time with undergraduates.) Faculty advisors have to teach, serve on committees, give papers at professional conferences, and often struggle to find time to tend to their own scholarship, the love of which is the reason they got into this business in the first place.

With that being said, just about every college now offers each incoming student some kind of an advisor or two at the outset, and some offer many. In most cases, a first-year is assigned an initial advisor sometime over the summer. That means that there are people on college campuses spending time purposefully matching incoming students to advisors. They may have a computer program to do it, they may do it by hand, or they may have a hybrid process that involves both. Some colleges even have one or several people who labor over this process for weeks.

Regardless of the method of assigning advisors to advisees, it is naturally impossible for anyone to predict whether or not an individual is going to click with an advisor in such a way that the advising experience will be a productive one. Plus, the advising system may or may not allow for switches. This is an essential point, and one that many students and parents do not realize until much later on, when perhaps disappointment, anger, and frustration at the advisors and the advising program have built up. What happens if that is the case for your child? Can a new advisor be assigned? How? You may want to understand how easy or hard it is to switch advisors and to learn about some of the finer points of the advising system before finalizing your decision. Not that this would be a deal breaker, but it might add a pro or con to your list.

Understanding Academic Advising at the Last Few Schools on Your List

Find the information on academic advising at your prospective colleges and bookmark the pages for future reference. Note how easy or difficult they were to find.

- Who are the academic advisors (faculty and/or staff)?
- How does the college match advisees to advisors?

- When do you find out who your child's advisor will be?
- Are the advisors available over the summer for conversation? For questions?
- When is the first meeting with the advisor?
- Are there mandatory meetings?
- How does a student set up an appointment? By phone, email, an app?
- How should an advisee prepare for the first meeting?
- What is the URL of the advising resources page? And what is listed there?
- Are there peer advisors? Are they assigned, or is there a pool of them to choose from? How do you find them and make appointments with them? Where do they meet with students?
- What other advising resources are on hand? Handbooks, FAQs, videos, tutorials?
- After a student declares a major/minor, who is available to advise on degree requirements? Do the full-time faculty in the major/minor department do that?
- Are the expectations of advisors and advisees clearly articulated?
- Are the advisors evaluated? Are the assessments on the website?

Of all the questions to consider in the list above, pay particular attention to whether or not a college's advisors are evaluated. If they are not evaluated, how are you supposed to know how good they are and how well they are meeting the needs and desires of their students? Assessing the work of advisors is an essential and fundamental exercise that indicates to the advisor what they are doing well and what they need to change going forward. It also signals to the advisors and the student body that advising is taken seriously. I know many schools where you are welcome to serve as a freshman advisor if you are (1) employed by the university and (2) breathing. At most campuses, advisors are winging it. Most do not evaluate advisors, and even fewer share the results.

Advising is hard work. Advisors have to prepare for it, learn rules and regulations, and pay attention to the ever-changing curricula, policies, and procedures. It takes time. The best systems are those that have advisors who are:

- Accessible
- Knowledgeable
- Approachable
- Caring

In national surveys and research, these are the main things students indicate are most important to them. How do you know whether or not your child's prospective colleges have advisors who meet all of those criteria? Unless the college publishes or will share with you the evaluations that previous students have done of advisors, then you do not know for sure.

Any college that offers incoming students professional staff *and* faculty *and* peers as advisors is working hard to maximize the opportunities for students to connect substantively with someone. All of them can be sounding boards, good listeners to help students pave their individual roads. They should also be able to tell students when they are heading down a path that will prevent them from reaching their goals and graduating on time. This can be tricky, depending on their potential interests.

Often students complain that they get different answers to a question depending on whom they ask. Universities are complex, and there are many paths to a given end. The messy reality of advising systems at colleges across the nation is that it is up to the student to establish their own board of advisors, people they come to trust, who have their best interests at heart, and who can easily say "I don't know, but let me help you find the answer" when appropriate.

I encourage every freshman to start immediately to build their own team of sounding boards. Of course, this is much easier said than done. Students are not used to having to construct their own team, so to speak. It's an entirely new concept. But in college, there are new rules and unexpected opportunities. The future is largely unknown. The lack of a clear formula for getting to the next step is unsettling. But there is never just one way to do any one thing. In fact, there are millions of possibilities. Each advisor will try to help students chart their own pathways. That's why a good advisor will elicit your child's story, not just once, but many times over the course of an advising relationship.

The other day I was in a clothing store and started talking to a young saleswoman named Rebecca who was helping me with some purchases. It turned out that she was a student at Tufts studying international relations, so of course I asked her about her advising experience. She said it was horrible. That's the usual response, so I probed a bit. She said that, yes, she had an advisor, and yes, she knew about all of the sources of information, but she didn't want to "tell her story" to one source of advice after another. She had told it once and felt that that was enough. She viewed college advising as a one-stop shopping experience. And she wanted that one advisor to tell her how to finish college fully prepared for a career in international relations. She wanted a clear formula to get her to the next step, just as she had had in high school. And she wanted to get all of her advising from one person. I suggested gently that she might want to get used to "telling her story" because we do it all our lives, and it can be fun. Every time we tell it there is something new to add, and we can change not only the perception others have of us but our self-perception a little bit each time. Telling your story is an opportunity for creating your story, a moment of growth and change.

Put plainly, college is anything but formulaic. But students like Rebecca arrive on campus expecting a formula for the next step. *How do I get a job on Wall Street? How do I get into medical school? Law school? Business school? How do I ensure success in the field of international relations?* And therefore many students don't see the value in the sort of exploratory advising relationships colleges have in mind when they talk about good advising.

Establishing a board of advisors at college is analogous to something we all do eventually. As adults, we have relationships based on trust with all kinds of people who assist with various aspects of our lives—an accountant for taxes, a financial advisor for money matters, a dentist for good oral health, physicians to manage health problems, a mechanic to fix the car, a gardener to tend the lawn, a lawyer for legal issues, a jeweler for a high-quality ring or watch. The list is endless. Likewise, we can think of college as the beginning of setting up trusting relationships with people who help us manage our life and make the best decisions at every turn. I am belaboring this point because knowing where to find guidance can make the difference between staying in school and not.

Case in point: Having completed her third semester, Alice felt lost and had no idea where to turn for help. She was seriously contemplating leaving college. Her parents panicked at the thought, and immediately wrote to the university's president, who connected the family with the head of advising. Alice's was a familiar story, so she invited Alice in for a conversation about her current situation. Over a ninety-minute conversation, they mapped out ways she could finish one of her top two majors of interest and one or two minors so that she could graduate with her class. Alice felt renewed hope as she headed home for the holidays. When the advisor circled back to the parents, with Alice's permission, they were relieved.

Advising conversations like this happen all of the time. They help ensure that students know how to access resources to have a great academic and nonacademic experience. Your child is about to enter a whole new world with a class full of other first-year students who don't know the landscape any better than they do. So they will need escorts through the new environment. That's why colleges do or should spend a lot of time and money on advising resources. In fact, I subscribe to the viewpoint that there are hundreds of advisors on every college campus because everyone who works there is ostensibly committed to the success and education of each student. Essentially, college is a place where a student needs to be resourceful to find guidance, advice, and mentoring in lots of different places. Knowing that, your child will be able to establish a crackerjack team of advisors.

Aligning Advising Expectations

With your child, write down what you expect from a college advisor. Compare that to the mission and vision of the advising office at the potential campuses. Are there differences between your expectations and those the college sets for the advising system?

No matter what the structure of a college's advising resources, advising is not a "one-stop shopping experience," as Rebecca had hoped. There are innumerable places to "get advising": faculty and professional advisors, residential advisors, peer advisors, career services, internship and study-abroad offices, financial aid counselors, research offices, departmental administrators, teaching assistants, research heads, et cetera. And then there are the unexpected, serendipitous places—the lab tech who ends up being an indispensable source of counsel, the teaching fellow whose life offers inspiration, the Spanish professor with whom your child might develop a profound connection, a harpsichord teacher who makes a student see the world differently. In other words, your child may encounter people who are not "assigned" the job of advising but who nevertheless may have a meaningful impact on a student's time in and beyond college.

Other Campus Support: Medical, Psychological, Wellness, and Disability Considerations

Colleges are communities in and of themselves that offer their students a variety of amenities. Especially given the national trend of skyrocketing mental health issues in this age group, an essential aspect of campus life is ensuring that students can maintain their health and well-being. But colleges differ in the resources they can and do dedicate to medical, psychological, wellness, and disability needs.

Student health services usually offer medical assistance for minor issues. Handily, many also do vaccinations!

Psychological support is often offered in the form of short- or long-term one-on-one or group therapy.

Wellness initiatives are proactive educational and inspirational campaigns and offerings that encourage students to live in the healthiest possible ways.

The disabilities services office is staffed by the person or people who will become a lifeline if your child has or suspects they have a disability and needs accommodations.

The first three are optional. Your prospective colleges may have some, lots of, or no medical, psychological, and wellness facilities. Health services may offer students, faculty, and staff medical assistance and/or psychological therapy and/or education initiatives. Wellness initiatives are designed to proactively encourage healthy living, but many colleges dedicate few resources to them. Good ones are expensive. Some of the most popular are:

- Mandated smoke-free campus and smoking-cessation programs
- Mind-body classes (meditation, yoga, tai chi)
- Nutritional information for dining hall foods plus options that incorporate hormone-free dairy products, locally sourced produce, and humanely raised meats
- Gluten-free, vegan, allergy-aware, kosher, halal, and vegetarian meals

- Community wellness challenges, such as races or walkathons
- Massage, acupuncture, chiropractic, Reiki, and other treatment modalities
- Outdoor adventure
- Organic farms and/or farmers' markets on campus or nearby
- Sustainability and environmental awareness
- Workshops on healthy life choices
- A fitness center that is large enough for the community, accessible, open long hours, and staffed with fitness experts knowledgeable about campus health offerings
- Sexual health promotion
- Peer education programs on everything from stress-reduction to LGBTQA life to men's health to healthy lifestyle choices
- Low- or no-fee physical education classes for the surrounding community
- Intramural and club sports

Most colleges are trying to meet a lot of needs on pretty tight budgets.

Disabilities accommodations are, on the other hand, not optional. They are regulated by federal law, so every college must have a way to adjudicate requests for accommodations, which can be provided in-house or by an external contractor. It is important to investigate the offerings on each of the prospective campuses if your son or daughter has been diagnosed with or may have a disability of any sort that is covered under the Americans with Disabilities Act.

Disability services staff review relevant documentation and determine the appropriate accommodations. These could be physical disabilities (such as those involving vision, ambulation, hearing, or concussions), learning disabilities (e.g., reasoning, speech, writing), or psychological disabilities (depression, bipolar disorder, et cetera). There's not always a bright line among these categories.

Regardless of whether or not your child has a known issue at this time, discovering a college's offerings with respect to physical and mental health, wellness, and disabilities is revealing. Parents and students often believe, quite falsely but understandably, that colleges have a wider array of services than they do. Keep in mind that the pressures on the healthcare system at any college or university are colossal. Consider just the number of students who battle depression during their college or graduate school years; it hovers at about one in two. If a college clinic has to treat half of its student body on an ongoing basis, it needs an outsized staff. Most schools cannot afford to provide long-term therapy to that many people, so they will offer a limited number of visits before referring students to local practitioners for longer-term care.

Focusing on Health Resources

Explore the college websites for information on medical, psychological, wellness, and disabilities initiatives. You will immediately be able to discern what sorts of resources are dedicated to each of these areas on the prospective campuses.

Consider Dan, a very successful high school football player, who attended a high school that offered him a vast array of disabilities accommodations based on the battery of tests he had taken in the eighth grade, which revealed an attention deficit disorder. Throughout high school he had note takers in his classrooms, extended time on all of his exams, tutors for each class, homework assistance for some subjects, and an exemption from the foreign language requirement. When he was recruited to play football, he and his family assumed that the college would provide the same level of assistance. Being proactive, his mother called the disabilities services office in April and shared with the staff member the list of accommodations her son would need in college. In that first conversation, she was distraught to learn that (1) Dan would have to have a new battery of tests, as the college would not accept test results that were more than three years old; (2) it was highly unusual for students to receive a foreign-language exemption, though Dan would surely be considered for it; (3) though Dan could arrange to get tutors, he would have to pay for their services, as they would not be provided as a disability accommodation; (4) the same kind of homework assistance would not be permitted; (5) now that Dan was eighteen, he would have to initiate the request to register with the office himself, and the parents' request could not be honored. Dan's mother felt as if the bloom had suddenly fallen off the proverbial rose. She had been so elated at the prospect of becoming part of this community. Now she felt dejected, betrayed, and upset on behalf of her son.

Students and parents should never assume that the accommodations they received in high school will match those in college because the two types of educational institutions are governed by different laws. High schools must comply with the Individuals with Disabilities Education Act (IDEA), which is designed for student *success*. Colleges, on the other hand, are beholden to the Americans with Disabilities Act (ADA), which is intended to ensure *access*. In other words, colleges are required to make accommodations that give all students equal entrée to the academic curriculum. They do not have to modify course materials, tests, or assignments to guarantee success. And any personal needs, such as transportation or personal care attendants, may have to be provided by the student. The institution is not compelled to provide such services.

If your child has ever been diagnosed with a disability of any sort, whether learning, psychological, or physical, you should immediately consult with the colleges on the types of documentation they need. If your child's tests are several years old, ask how current they have to be. If you wait until August to have new ones done, you almost certainly will not have the report in time for fall accommodations to be put in place. The whole process from beginning to end can take months. And any grades your child receives before those accommodations are in place cannot be changed. Keep in mind that the college or university will probably not pay for testing, which can be expensive and time-consuming. Most don't offer financial aid to cover it, though there may be a fund students can access via an application process.

An important reminder: If your child will be eighteen when entering college, you—the parents—cannot access their grades or disabilities records without the student's written consent. The corollary to this is that it is your eighteen-year-old's responsibility to notify the relevant college office of a potential or actual disability. Your child may also be the one who has to notify each professor every semester of their accommodations, and parental input is definitely not welcomed there. Many colleges deem it important for students to learn how to advocate for themselves. So your child may have to be his own spokesperson to receive the assistance in coursework you or they think they need.

Another difference from high school is that your child will be required to manage their own time and do a lot of independent work. Nationally, students ought to spend about three hours studying outside of class for every credit hour in the classroom. The lack of structure and the amount of independent work can be daunting to every student, and even more so for students with particular disabilities.

My advice is to contact disabilities services as soon as possible if your child has a diagnosed or suspected disability that may warrant accommodations. This is nothing to blow off or ignore; doing so can be a recipe for disaster. If this is particularly important to you, look at the Additional Resources section for two books solely dedicated to the transition from high school to college for students with disabilities.

Pre-deposit Considerations

Now is the time to ask again—and figure out—if your child's potential schools align with her or his academic and non-academic interests, and are big or small enough.

- It is revealing to investigate the real story of faculty access and availability in the crucial first two years.
- Spending a few minutes investigating the options for study abroad or study away is a good use of your time.
- Figuring out who the advisors will be and how easily a student can switch can be very telling.
- Colleges and universities differ in their abilities to provide medical, wellness, and disability services.

The Campus Community

Now that you have the essential information about the structure and composition of the college or university, the likelihood that your child will have substantive interaction with full-time faculty members, the options for study abroad, and the support structures in place, you are in a much better position not only to make a final decision but also to align your expectations with the campus offerings. It's time to turn your attention to the out-of-classroom life of the college, just so you can take a peek at some of the tantalizing—or not so alluring—opportunities that await your child.

Every campus has its own DNA, and student social life is a contributing factor to that uniqueness. It is created by its past and current students, faculty, and administrators. In the absence of experiencing a campus, people are tempted to think that institutions in the same "tier" resemble one another. It's not uncommon for parents and students alike to imagine that all of the Ivy League schools are similar, but this is far from true. Likewise, you might be tempted to think that Smith, Mount Holyoke, Amherst, Hampshire, and the University of Massachusetts at Amherst resemble one another a great deal. After all, they belong to a five-college consortium, and the campuses are linked by a bus system designed to enable students to take courses at any of them, regardless of where they matriculate.

But the student experience at each school is quite different. It's hard to put your finger on what all of the differences are, but two very important distinctions, in addition to the size of the student body and numbers of faculty members, are the makeup of the student body and the components of undergraduate social life. Students spend only twelve to twenty hours a week in class, so the vast majority of their time, the other 148 to 156 hours, will be spent elsewhere. When they are not in a lecture, seminar, or lab, they will (hopefully) be engaging in some of the activities the campus offers, where they will meet peers, develop interests, and forge connections, some of which will last a lifetime.

To Do

Learn about the makeup of the student body of the schools still on your child's list. How many states and countries are represented among the undergraduates? What percentage comes from the area in which the college is located? What is the gender makeup? What about the ethnic composition? Do most of the students come from public or private high schools? What about socioeconomic diversity? Does the college list the percentage of first-generation students and the services offered to this crucial group? Most of these data points and more are handily available at CollegeData.com.

This is a complex topic, but naturally, a college student body benefits its students a great deal when it mirrors the world in which we live. After all, living for four years in a microcosm of our society will offer valuable lessons about working and playing in the broader society. The world is nothing if not diverse, with almost two hundred countries and seven thousand languages. College graduates may well wind up working in industries and organizations that do not even exist yet, with people from around the globe. The best education will be one that prepares every student for the wildly exciting variety of human experience they will enjoy their whole lives.

In the long term, the people your child meets at college will become colleagues in future workplaces, friends they go on vacation with and visit in their hometowns, and connections they will use whenever they seek whatever it is that they need or want. If your son's best friend from college lives in Paris, he may have a place to stay when he is there. If the majority of his friends have roots in the local area, he will have a built-in network to build on if he starts his career there.

In the shorter term, the ethnic and racial makeup of the student body will, to some extent, define the organized social offerings, meaning the clubs and organizations that students can join. If there is a large Latino or Hispanic population, it's possible that your child can learn salsa or other Latin-style dances. One of my very favorite students ever joined a Latino dance troupe in her freshman year, and it lives on in her memory as the place where she had the greatest sense of belonging, not to mention fun. She hailed from an all-white upper-middle-class New England town, so the affinity with this group was not a no-brainer. This is somewhat of an oversimplification, but it stands to reason that an ethnically and racially diverse community will offer its students more opportunities to experience a greater array of activities, opinions, and thoughts, ones that reflect the world more accurately than those that are relatively homogeneous.

What may be just as or even more important is the socioeconomic diversity of the student body. There is currently a big push on every college campus to make it as economically inclusive as possible. Institutions not only want to address the access and equity issues in our larger society but also want to offer their students a richer experience while on campus.

How would you go about figuring out whether your child's potential future schools are economically diverse or not? One measure that the experts often use is the percentage of the student body receiving Pell Grants. Pell-eligible families generally earn less than $60,000 (other factors play into the eligibility as well). *U.S. News & World Report* offers a handy table of all schools' Pell-eligible percentages.

Another measure of diversity is the percentage of first-generation college students, a statistic that some colleges are just beginning to display on their websites. First-gen students are those whose parents did not get a college degree—either at all or before the child was born. This population cuts across racial, ethnic, and socioeconomic lines, in fact, and brings a perspective to the classroom that helps others question assumptions, thereby enriching the conversation. This group has been in the news a lot lately because colleges boast about admitting them, but many institutions lack the scaffolding they need to get them to the degree. Organizations like FLIP (First-Generation Low-Income Partnership) raise awareness of and provide resources for students who fall into this category.

Whether your child is lesbian, gay, bisexual, transgender, questioning, an ally, or none of the above, this disparate group is increasingly visible and vocal on campuses across the country as well. Some staff large offices, who, together with faculty and/or professional staff, mount events, initiate awareness-raising campaigns, and create a supportive community for the education and betterment of everyone. Other campuses have fewer resources to dedicate to this cause. Either way, a quick look at the offerings will tell you a lot about the campus's abilities to support them, whether or not this is relevant to you and/or your child.

Another important factor in any campus social life is the range of clubs and organizations offered. Often, if a student has a burning passion to engage in a somewhat unusual activity, such as equestrian sports, juggling, aikido, or Afro-Caribbean dance, the question about organizations and clubs has loomed large in your search for a college. But more often, applicants have lots of general interests and assume that they can engage in any or all of them when they get to campus. Students and their parents are often crestfallen when they discover that the school lacks some key extracurriculars that would have tipped the scales if they had only thought to ask ahead of time.

If your child's top school does not offer the activity they are most interested in, you might think that's no problem—your child can just start a new club to cater to their interest. Unfortunately, no matter what the reassuring campus tour guide may have told you when you visited, founding an organization will be way more difficult than you think. On some campuses, it can take over a year, lots of paperwork, and no small amount of fortitude. So paying attention to the list of already existing extracurriculars is a good idea.

But there, too, you have to be careful. Colleges love to quote a large number of clubs and organizations. When you dig deeper, though, you will discover that many of them are inactive because they were initiated years ago by some fervent undergraduates only to die a quick death when those same students graduated. Few schools revise their online offerings on a regular basis, probably because it falls to the bottom of the never-ending priority list.

To figure out the options at your schools of interest, CollegeData is not too helpful either, as it merely lists categories of activities that are reported by the school. The only way to approach this question is to search the college website and scour the student newspaper for articles and ads pertaining to the groups that interest your child.

Let's do a little poking around. When investigating the site for Columbia University, for example, you notice that the Buddhist Meditation Group's link leads you to a webpage that has not been updated since 2005. That is a pretty good indication of its activity level. The same is the case for a group called HELLAS, the under-graduate Greek American organization. The page for Ho-Heup, a Korean drumming society, cites 2007 as its last active year. Hillel at Columbia/Barnard, on the other hand, has a completely up-to-date and extensive list of ways to get involved.

To Do

Find the webpage that lists existing clubs and organizations. Initially, you might be impressed by an enormous list. Now click on some of them and note the dates of last activity to determine which are truly active and which are not. If your child's interests are not represented by active groups, then find the webpage that describes the process for creating a new organization. Is a student committee in charge of the decision? Or an administrative office? Is funding available? How long does the process take? How many students have to be interested? Would they need a faculty or administrative advisor for the group?

Another example is the University of North Carolina at Chapel Hill, which says it has over eight hundred officially recognized student groups. If you click on a few, you will see how many members make up each group and get an indication of how active or inactive they are. The page spells out the guidelines for creating a new group very clearly in their Office of Student Organizations pages. The list of information the office requires is extensive. And again, the process probably takes longer than most undergraduates want to wait, even if they're really interested in starting their own group.

That raises a question: Why seek official recognition at all? Couldn't students just start something on their own without university acknowledgment? The reason most students need the college's

approval is, first and foremost, to qualify for funding (which is normally monies collected by the school from students in the form of
"student fees" in the bill you receive every term). Second, and sometimes equally important, is the ability to use other university resources to run the group (space reservations, webpages, et cetera).
Without official recognition, they can't reserve meeting rooms, theaters, practice areas, or performance spaces, and students themselves
have to bear the cost of advertising and putting on their events.

I emphasize extracurriculars because research has shown that
students learn a great deal outside of coursework, and their extracurricular activities are particularly important in this regard. In fact,
Richard Light, a Harvard researcher who's a rock star in the world of
higher education, says: "The evidence shows that . . . learning outside of classes, especially in residential settings and extracurricular
activities such as the arts, is vital. When we asked students to think
of a specific, critical incident or moment that had changed them pro-
foundly, four-fifths of them chose a situation or event outside of the
classroom." If 80 percent of students acknowledge in retrospect that
something outside of the classroom offered them the most significant experience of their undergraduate lives, doing the research before finalizing the decision is definitely worth the time.

Does Social Life = Greek Life?

The social life at some colleges famously takes place at houses that
belong to fraternities and sororities. At others, students barely notice
the existence of these so-called Greek organizations. It pays to be
aware ahead of time how much of the undergraduate social life is
dominated by them. Some students are sure they want to join one;
others want to avoid them like the plague. For students who are interested in them, they can provide a superb lifelong social network.
For those who would prefer to avoid them, they can be an annoy-
ingly dominant force on campus. Here are some of the pros and cons
of joining them:

Pros of Greek Organizations

- They provide a network of friends and acquaintances who are interested in a similar social, academic, civic, or religious life.
- They can become a major part of a student's social life, providing a sort of built-in circle of friends in a community in which they otherwise may not know anyone at first.
- This network can last a lifetime and can be extraordinarily helpful in future job searches, in social life, and even when settling into a new town or city.
- Some of these organizations do impressive community service or help members hone particular skills, such as writing or developing financial portfolios.

Cons of Greek Organizations

- They may limit a student's social network to those in the fraternity or sorority to some extent.
- Greek organizations can cost money during recruitment and in future dues, social events, and outings.
- Many fraternities and sororities are known to engage in excessive drinking, which can infamously reach dangerous levels.
- Some of these organizations involve extensive hazing rituals, which are illegal in many states and can be physically risky.

How do you figure out how much of the social life on the future potential campuses is determined by Greek life? *U.S. News & World Report* lists those schools at which 25 percent or more of students belong to Greek organizations. You will note in this list that on some campuses over 70 percent of students belong to fraternities or sororities. That may be a draw for you and your child or it may not. It really comes down to personal preference. Additionally, under the heading "Campus Life," CollegeData lists the percentages of students who belong to these groups. However, this is not 100 percent foolproof. DePauw University in Greencastle, Indiana, does not have any percentage listed on CollegeData, but *U.S. News & World Report* says that over 75 percent of students there belong to a Greek organization.

To make things even more complicated, all of these numbers can be deceiving. If you look at the University of Indianapolis and at Princeton University, the data state that 100 percent of the students on both campuses are "independent." You may think this means that no students there belong to a fraternity or a sorority. However, what this actually means is that the institutions do not officially acknowledge the existence of Greek groups. They do not support them, negotiate with them, or provide them any facilities whatsoever. But they actually exist on those campuses! To find out the real story, you will have to do more digging.

As it turns out, Princeton has, in fact, very little Greek life because campus social life is dominated by the eating clubs that line Prospect Avenue in this little New Jersey town. These are independent institutions, with governing boards of often wealthy alumni, that charge their members high fees. These stunning mansions are the dining halls for most juniors and seniors as well, so students pay for their dining plans here, too. If you look a bit more deeply, you will learn that some of them are "bicker" clubs, which means that students have to go through a very stressful (and often humiliating) process to gain acceptance, and admission is up to a group of existing club members. Others are "sign-in" clubs, welcoming all comers—and therefore carry significantly less prestige. But they all cost something to join and remain in good standing. To find out how many students conduct their social lives on "the Street," as Prospect Avenue is known, my suggestion would be to seek out advice on College Confidential or scour the student newspaper (which is funded in part by the university, so it's not completely independent). I would not ask tour guides, as they are trained to answer such questions with a positive spin. If while making their decision your child can spend a day or night on campus during the official events for admitted students, they will learn everything they need to know about the social life in real time by hanging out with and asking questions of current students.

The story at the University of Indianapolis is quite different. It is a so-called dry campus, with very strict rules about alcohol usage. In fact, it is a zero-tolerance school, and there doesn't appear to be much of a party life at all.

For students who are not interested in joining a fraternity or sorority or eating club (or the equivalent), it is important to find out what alternatives exist. How do other students find a community? Is it possible? Probable? Current students are the best sources of this sort of information. If you post a question like this on Facebook, you should be aware that students who answer may be employed by the admission office. You want to be sure you get the real scoop from students who are not being paid by the university. Sometimes the only way to find out is to ask random enrolled students when you visit the campus on those days designed to woo admitted students. Hearing the views of a number of them, not just one, will be telling. You don't want the only person you ask to be a student who hates the place and is working on a transfer application. I wouldn't be shy. Remembering that you are about to commit a lot of money and time to the place will help. Ask a bunch of students, advisors, and faculty, and you will inevitably get the real story. What's true is that *every* campus is trying to hide at least one thing, if not multiple things, from prospective students. Finding out what that is ahead of time will help!

Admitted Students Days

The best questions to ask students who are not tour guides and not otherwise on the college payroll:

- What do you wish you had known before you came to campus?
- Did anything surprise you about this college?
- What advice would you give an incoming freshman?
- If you had to do it all over again, would you have come here? If so, why? If not, why not?

Religion and Spirituality on Campus

If your child is religious, the campus religious offerings and culture have likely loomed large in your search. If not, then a quick look at the services can be illuminating. It stands to reason that young people are invested in understanding what life is all about and how they should invest their energy as a participant on the planet. A number of years ago, a UCLA research group, Spirituality in Higher Education, confirmed that "today's college students have very high levels of spiritual interest and involvement. Many are actively engaged in a spiritual quest and are exploring the meaning and purpose of life. They also display high levels of religious commitment and involvement." Whether a college is in a rural, suburban, or urban area, it surely has something like an Office of Religious Life that is responsible for connecting the campus community with religious leaders in the surrounding communities to offer support and observance to students. In some locations, of course, it will be harder to find representatives of smaller religious communities. But rabbis, pastors, imams, priests, and other faith leaders will go to great lengths to connect with and serve university communities as their chaplains. At a small suburban campus, however, an imam or Sikh Granthi may only be able to come to campus once a week because they are traveling to many different locales on the other days of the week. Take a look at the offerings at Grinnell College's Center for Religion, Spirituality, and Social Justice for a stellar example of a wealth of resources. These offices work not only to support the religious and spiritual members of the communities but also to offer programs and initiatives that enhance the entire community. They can be effective leaders in times of campus difficulties or regional and national tragedies as well.

The Political Dynamic

Another factor that plays a big part in determining the complexion of a campus is the political leanings of the student body and faculty. Especially given the partisan split of our country, if the campus is largely conservative and Republican, the experience is going to be very different than if the campus is largely liberal and Democratic. For example, recently many conservative-leaning students have complained in the student press about the lack of diversity of political opinions among faculty members on their campuses. Some students have felt silenced in conversation and disdained by their teachers. Conservative faculty members often feel ostracized by their liberal colleagues on many campuses.

I'm not suggesting that conservatives should choose conservative campuses and liberals seek out only like-minded colleges. I have known conservative students who chose to pursue a degree at a liberal college and vice versa. These students reason wisely and correctly that having their ideas challenged over time is the best way to fortify them and to practice articulating them for a future career—for example, in politics. On very liberal campuses, there are also usually pockets of more conservative students who knit together a strong social and career-networking group that serves them well throughout their entire lives.

There are lists of the most liberal and most conservative colleges, but many fall somewhere in between and will offer every politically engaged student more than one option in terms of activities and extracurriculars, and wide exposure to a vast array of political ideas both in and outside of classrooms. It is important, however, not to assume this, but rather to be informed before choosing.

Related, but not exactly the same, is the question of whether a campus is known for this or not. Social activism and a left-leaning political stance are in the very genetic material of some campuses. Especially now when colleges are lit up by activists demanding change with respect to racial, socioeconomic, and gender-based issues, it is important to be aware of the college's historical and current activist activities. If a student chooses Reed College, Oberlin, the University of Vermont, or Kenyon, for example, then they will have a wealth of opportunities to learn about and participate in grassroots efforts to direct and promote societal reform. These campuses draw faculty members who weave the history, theories, and principles of cultural and social change into their course materials. In places like these, the call to be socially conscious and engaged is ubiquitous and absolutely cannot be ignored. As exciting as this might be for some, it can wear on students who don't want that to dominate conversation and activities.

The first big wave of social activism on U.S. college campuses came in the late 1960s, when students effected tremendous political shifts in the American landscape with respect to sexual mores, the Vietnam War, civil rights, apartheid, and nuclear proliferation. It is not uncommon to hear people these days compare the fervency of today's students with that of the students of five decades ago. Historians, the media, pundits, and others look on with great anticipation to see how much power today's students will garner on the national political landscape. If your child prefers to be on such a campus or, conversely, to avoid this kind of activity at all costs, this can be a determining factor in the decision.

Musical Considerations

If your child plays an instrument but does not plan to major in music, ask how non-majors can take lessons and join orchestras, chamber groups, choruses, and bands. Be prepared to find that these things can be both frustratingly difficult to find and expensive. Most schools charge extra for music lessons, above and beyond tuition and other fees, and students have to audition to qualify. Storage space for musical instruments can also be hard to come by. If this is high on your kid's list, take a look!

De-stressing in the Campus Gym

Your child may have applied to a particular set of schools because they *want* to play an organized sport and may even have been recruited. If so, then you have already considered the athletic facilities in great detail. But if your child doesn't fall into that category, exercise and/or playing a club or intramural sport may still become a really important part of their college social life. You may want to pause a moment to consider this more thoroughly than last year's cursory tour of the gym allowed, because the lack of adequate gym facilities is a source of constant annoyance for many undergraduates. If this is important to your child, you can easily find out if this is something current students are happy with or complain about. The key question is how crowded the gym and pools are at peak times, such as right after afternoon classes and before dinner hours. If the answer is "Very," you will want to find out if the school has contracted with local gyms to offer students reduced-rate memberships. The best way to glean all of this information may be to ask on College Confidential or on the college's social media sites, if your child is permitted to post there as an accepted student, or on the parent portal, if one is offered. Again, this is also something you can find out when you visit during Admitted Students Days, but, again, official tour guides are not necessarily going to be as honest as you would like. Find students who are relaxing somewhere in the student union or cafeteria and see if they will give a few minutes of their time so you can get the real story.

Second, if your child has an interest in learning new physical activities, take a look at the range of offerings, and inquire about the feasibility of freshmen and sophomores taking them. Regardless of whether the popular sports are racquetball and swimming, yoga and tennis, or scuba diving and Zumba, it can be next to impossible to sign up for these classes until your child has an earlier registration time. First-year students have the lowest priority in the registration lineup, so they register *after* the sophomores, juniors, and seniors have already signed up for their fall classes the previous spring (though some colleges judiciously set aside seats in fall courses for incoming students). Obviously, in these situations, nabbing a spot in popular classes will get easier from year to year.

At approximately 30 percent of colleges, physical education is still required to graduate, though the number of those schools is decreasing. Regardless of whether or not it is required, some physical education courses carry additional fees, above and beyond tuition and other costs. Scuba diving, skiing, and sailing, for example, can be pretty expensive on many campuses.

Here are some additional things to be aware of.

- At schools with a PE requirement, varsity athletes may be able to fulfill the PE requirement through participation in their sports. Pay close attention to the procedure for getting credit!
- Schools usually have special rules regarding ROTC students' fulfillment of a PE requirement.
- At many liberal arts colleges, PE classes do not count toward a degree. At many other schools, the number of credits that will count is limited.

- The registration process for PE classes may be different from that for other courses. Students should pay close attention to the procedures and deadlines.
- There is a difference between varsity sport participation, PE classes, and so-called club sports, which are more informal, school-supported groups designed for fun. Schools generally will not count club sport participation toward a PE or credit requirement.
- If your child plans to participate in a club sport, ask about the club's insurance coverage. This is particularly important for very active sports like rugby and Ultimate Frisbee, for example.
- If your child has a serious interest in a sport that is not offered, you might suggest that they talk to the head of the PE department or the athletic director to see if there is any possibility that a new course can be mounted in the coming years.
- Some schools charge an athletics fee every semester, regardless of whether students use the facilities or not. Some schools charge a flat fee for PE courses per year (or per semester), while at others the price is variable depending on the sport or class.
- If you are assessed a fee for a PE class and your child decides to drop it, you may not get a refund. Strict deadlines for dropping these classes usually apply.
- If a PE course (or any course) is dropped after a certain deadline, it may still appear on the transcript. Students need to pay close attention to the drop deadlines or risk accruing an incomplete, something like a W (for withdrawn), or a failing mark.
- Some PE classes have strict attendance policies. Students really do not want an F in a PE class on the transcript, so it is good to be aware of these policies. There may be opportunities to make up classes if they miss some, but there may not.
- Even if your child has a well-developed interest in a particular activity, some schools do not permit students to count a PE class more than once toward the requirement or degree.

- Some PE activities, like scuba diving, will require medical certification ahead of time, so you may want to start this process early.
- If your child has a physical disability that you believe will exempt them from PE, begin by submitting documentation to the office that handles disability services as soon as possible. This process may take longer than you would imagine. Estimate how long you think it should take and then triple it to be safe. Disability services offices are usually miserably understaffed, and they have high burnout rates and turnover. Most schools will not let students out of the requirement completely but will instead create an appropriate accommodation.

All of these policies and procedures should be easy to find in the college handbook. Reading that document from end to end will probably take less than an hour and can spare you disappointment, prevent the transcript from bearing unwanted indicators of course withdrawals, and save you money in the end.

Dorm Life

While it is tempting to think of social life and residential life as one and the same, colleges think of them as distinctly different. The former is made up of all the things discussed above that make up the students' interactions outside of the classroom and dorm. The latter is made up of the buildings designed to house students and the initiatives mounted to enhance their lives. Your child's experiences in their home away from home will be affected by the people who live there and the intentional programs and events on offer there. Residential life can be very structured, rule-bound, and organized, or it may be loose and more catch-as-catch-can. Knowing who is living on campus and which mandatory and optional initiatives are created by the school for the benefit of students living there can be important in your final decision-making process.

On Campus Versus Off Campus

Many colleges require students to live in their residence halls the first year, some require it the first two years, and others require residential-hall/on-campus living for all four. At the other end of the spectrum are the colleges that have few dormitories, so only a small percentage of students live on campus at all the first year and the rest rent from local landlords or live at home. (In some cases, dormitories are more cost effective; in others, they are more costly than living in town.) CollegeData provides some of the information you need on this aspect of college life.

Requiring all freshmen and sophomores to live on campus means there will be mandatory programs like RA meetings and bystander training where students learn to help others out of potentially precarious social situations. Optional educational and social programs will span the gamut from faculty dinners and peer advisor teas to running clubs, theater outings, and hiking trips.

This is important to you as a parent because colleges that provide their students with homes and programming have higher retention rates and happier alumni. Becoming a member of the institution's social fabric helps students develop a deeper connection to their college. The more connected they feel, the more they will invest in building a life there, and the greater the probability that they will finish a degree, become alumni donors, and not end up one of the 50 percent of students who do not make it to the bachelor's. Some of the programs may seem cumbersome and boring, but they are the college's attempt to engage and invest in students. If your child does not like what is on offer, it is likely that they can easily figure out how to contribute to the development and implementation of future initiatives. Most colleges are dying for student input and energy and will gladly give your child a chance to mold future initiatives in substantive ways.

The Roommate Situation

At most schools, the overwhelming majority of freshmen share a room. This is not always the case, however. Two of the undergraduate schools at Columbia University offer singles to 80 percent of incoming freshmen. Students therefore have two semesters to get to know people well enough to choose their roommates for the sophomore year, when most students have to double or triple up or find enough roommates for a suite. Some people like this, and it surely reduces the number of roommate conflicts the residential staff have to deal with the first year. But other people prefer to share rooms so that they have a sometime companion at the ready.

The truth is that most freshmen have to double or triple up at least. Housing is so short on many campuses that they are making triples out of doubles and quadruples out of triples. Some states have a minimum number of square feet of space for each student. New Jersey, for example, has legislated that each student be provided with 70 square feet for the first occupant and 50 square feet for each additional, so it is possible that the College of New Jersey or Rutgers University will have three students living in 170 square feet and four living in 220. That makes for pretty cozy living!

And then there are the lengthy lists of colleges that only guarantee housing for one or two years. After that, students are on their own, so you may well find yourself dealing with local landlords in the future and haggling with them about nine-month as opposed to twelve-month leases. In these cases, see if there is an off-campus housing office that vets and advertises local properties and perhaps even helps students who encounter difficulties. Colleges usually can't dedicate resources to this, but students end up figuring this out together pretty successfully.

Residential Advisors, Learning Communities, and Themed Living

If a campus requires students to live on campus for any period of time, it also spends a considerable amount of time and money hiring and training resident advisors (RAs) to live in the halls to guide students, provide a sympathetic ear, and organize programs. These are the students to whom first-years, in particular, tend to turn in the middle of the night when they are feeling unbearably lonely or homesick or cannot figure out how to get into the economics class they are dying to take. Some RAs also play an official role in the college's disciplinary process, which makes it awkward if your child suddenly gets written up for an infraction by the person to whom they have disclosed some of their deepest fears. The ratios of RAs to students can vary from just a handful of students per RA to several dozen. This ratio is an indicator of how available an RA can be to your child if they are in need of a shoulder to cry on or quick academic advice. It is also one measure of how committed the college is to cultivating a rich residential life. Consider Kalamazoo College in Michigan, for example, where there are 1,450 undergraduates, most of whom live in college dorms. All of the 350 or so freshmen are assigned to one of three residences, and each hall has four RAs, which means the ratio is approximately thirty students to every RA. That's a pretty typical number because it serves the students well.

It is also interesting to note what sorts of so-called living-learning communities are offered through the residential life office. These are clusters of rooms dedicated to housing students who share a particular interest, like engineering, scientific research, sober living, social activism, religion, LGBTQA issues, civic engagement, creative writing, premed, or a vegan lifestyle, just to name a few. Some colleges call them "theme housing," such as Wheaton College in Massachusetts, which offers a large number of such options for its 1,650 undergraduates. The University of Louisville in Kentucky gives housing priority to its 4,000 or so incoming freshmen but does not house all of them. However, it offers some interesting living-learning possibilities for Army ROTC students, predental students, and even one all-male-themed community. These types of residences house a small number of students who cultivate their shared interests in a tight-knit community within the larger one. Some have RAs and some don't. Some have faculty advisors and faculty-led programs and some don't. The details of these kinds of communities vary and can determine whether this is an appealing option for your child. Getting in can be competitive, so some colleges set aside spaces for incoming students to ensure a mix of years in each residence. Yet others are only for older students.

Many undergraduate communities invite graduate students, faculty, deans, visiting artists and professors, or even community members and their families to join the undergraduate life in the residence halls. These additional adults not only offer support and productive interaction but help the dorm community resemble "real life" a teeny bit more. If housing is offered to non-undergraduates, the expectation is usually that these people will donate time to enhance the residence in some way, by holding study breaks, hosting dinners, or running educational programs of some sort. Their presence also helps tamp down some of the more exuberant activities of dorms that otherwise house just eighteen- to twenty-two-year-olds. Some colleges have graduate students in the undergraduate residences rather than faculty. And a few offer non-faculty community members housing in exchange for mounting fun and educational programs for students.

I always advise students to take advantage of these programs as frequently as possible. They are unique opportunities to spend time with grad students and other adults outside of the classroom, to learn about their interests and work, and to seek advice from someone who understands the academic enterprise but who is not grading you. Without the evaluative aspect of the relationship, students are free to seek these people out as true sounding boards, informal advisors, and mentors. Unfortunately, most students do not take advantage of these programs, and it is truly a missed opportunity. I would advise your child: If faculty offer dinners, sign up. If they want to take you hiking, go! If there's an excursion to a museum, take them up on it. These activities not only offer a break from the usual routine but can be the source of serendipitous insights, advice, fun, and future opportunities.

If your child's potential future colleges offer these, give them a check in the "pro" column. Beyond being great opportunities for undergraduates, they also signal the school's fundamental commitment to a holistic living and learning environment.

Other Ways to Assess the Character of Residential Life

Beyond faculty and other adults living in the halls to offer programming, residential life offices usually organize myriad options for residents. These range from open mike nights and cooking classes to club sports and literary magazines. Courses may even be offered in the residence halls, for credit or not. These activities lend the dorms character that distinguishes one from the other; likewise, they attract students who are interested in those undertakings, so like-minded students can find one another. Check to see if the residence halls have cafés where students organize performances, therapy-dog programs at homes for the aging, or a hockey team that hits the ice every morning at 5:00 A.M. Some dorms put together periodic scavenger hunts, game nights, and talent shows. Others have strong alumni programming, which can be invaluable in internship and job searches. Most have a student committee that has ample funds to distribute for dorm outings and other social or educational events.

Getting back to the basics about residential life, the most important questions to ask at this point are:

- What percentage of incoming students share rooms?
- What is the number of doubles, triples, quads, et cetera?

- How many rooms are in hallways versus suites versus something else?
- Have the first-year students' rooms been converted from doubles to triples or from triples to quads?
- What are the most common complaints about the housing?

I have known many students to adjust very quickly to whatever arrangement they are placed in, but I have known a small percentage that resist mightily. They use whatever means at their disposal to try to force the college to reassign them. This fails more often than it succeeds. Even if you engage a lawyer or doctor, unless your child has a documented, verifiable condition that is covered by the Americans with Disabilities Act, the college will likely resist moving a freshman.

Dorm Amenities

With the number of graduating high school seniors decreasing over time, colleges are sinking real money into their dorms to attract new students and keep them. From green or eco-friendly living to climbing walls and zip lines, from movies in the pools to full-on water parks, the race is truly on to get you and your child to say yes. See if your child's prospective college dorms have movie or black-box theaters, or studios for painting, photography, music, dance, ceramics, recording, or digital media. Some of these will only be available to students who live there; others open up these facilities to the whole community.

Food, Glorious Food!

Sustenance looms large in the life of most undergraduates. Luckily, colleges have come a long way since I fought to get my dining hall to institute the first-ever salad bar in the 1980s. Not only are parents and their children demanding a greater number of healthy options, but it has become a commonplace that healthier students mean better learners. BestColleges.com even publishes a list of the most outstanding college dining halls, giving clear preference to healthy options and sustainable practices. The number of schools forging relationships with local agricultural and food businesses to offer "farm to dining hall" meals is also skyrocketing, to the benefit of all involved, if not the parental pocketbook.

Parents often worry that colleges will not pay attention to an individual student's dietary requirements and restrictions, but in my experience, chefs and nutritionists bend over backward to cater to special needs. If your child falls into this category, reach out early to work with the staff. Look up the procedure for making special requests and find out if it has to be done every semester, what sort of documentation is needed, and from whom. I've known students with all kinds of allergies, from nuts to milk to fish to wheat, and many unfortunately wait until the last minute to work with the college staff dedicated to this. Colleges want your child to be safe and healthy, so they will take pains to ensure that medical essentials are met. Get started early.

What about cooking options? Dorm life is also regulated by insurance companies, so many do not permit cooking. At all. And if they do allow heat-producing appliances, they are very specific about which ones. Even the most benign coffee machine can be confiscated in one of Public Safety's unannounced inspections. And hefty fines might be charged. The college has a list of acceptable devices, and my advice is to pay attention to it before buying anything. There are actually good reasons to restrict student cooking, among which, first and foremost, is hygiene. But if your child needs their own brand of coffee first thing in the morning or, more seriously, has a food allergy that requires them to stay out of a facility where an allergen is even stored, these are questions that will guide your which-school decision.

Parents Wanted?

This is not going to make or break your perception of a college, but it is interesting to note that some campuses welcome and engage parents in ever more creative ways, and others (though decreasing in number) eschew their very presence from day one. If this is important to you, you may want to do the following:

- Go to the websites of your prospective colleges and see whether they have a parent and family programs office of some sort, and if so, what it offers.
- Is there a list of people for you to contact?
- Is there a handbook, a newsletter, a list of family events, handy advice, or interesting ways for parents to get involved?
- Which office is responsible? Is it Alumni Affairs and Development, Student Affairs, or Academic Affairs? (If it is a development office, then their primary activities will inevitably be the solicitation of funds to support the institution.)
- Pay particular attention to any guidelines or expectations they offer parents. These will serve as an indicator of the college's philosophy on the parents' role in the life of a college kid and may give you insight into the most common issues that have arisen there in the recent past.

What If Your Child Didn't Get In Where They Want to Go . . . or Wants to Take Some Time Off?

As horrifying as the possibility of not being accepted anywhere might seem, it does happen. After all, college admission is a numbers game. Sometimes the odds don't come out in your favor. And it can be devastating. If this happens to your child, there will be tears and anger and frustration and hurt feelings all around. The best thing you can do is to acknowledge those feelings—in yourself and your child—and give each of you some space to grapple with the emotions of rejection. One of the most frequent assumptions at this moment is that you have no options: your worst fear has been realized, and your child is destined to stumble in life because you have failed them as a parent.

When you are ready, at the risk of seeming too Pollyannaish, what you can do with conviction is to see the absence of an acceptance letter as a true opportunity. There are two main reasons for this. Of the over four thousand colleges in our country, quite a few have rolling admission, so this is a chance to take a look at some of the colleges you might not have previously considered. Just search the Web for the lists of schools with rolling admission, and begin exploring. I know you are tired, but if your child is bound and determined to go to college in the fall, this can be a practical, illuminating, and fortifying next step.

Before any new applications are sent, it is wise to call some of the admission offices that sent rejection letters and ask if there was anything about the submission that stood out to reviewers as a red flag. If they will be honest with you (and unfortunately many won't), it will help with future attempts to get that coveted acceptance letter. Don't call them directly after decisions have arrived; they need a few days to regroup, too. Admission officers work around the clock to get decisions out the door on time, so they are truly exhausted; waiting a few days will increase the likelihood of reaching someone who has the energy to care about your inquiry. They may say that they will only speak to applicants themselves, so be sure to engage your child in the process. If they want to initiate the call, all the better. But if they won't, they can hop on the phone if needed.

The second reason this is a true opportunity is that you and your child can now think seriously about a gap year. Yes, I said it: the two words parents react to with horror for fear that their child will never go to college if they don't go now. But this is the true silver lining right here.

Dozens if not hundreds of parents and students have asked me about the wisdom of a gap year. All are taken aback when I urge them adamantly to go for it. Why? Sue's son, Carl, offers a great example. He had been a good student in high school but had fallen into a pretty serious senior slump. He was thrilled to be admitted to his first-choice school, Stony Brook University, but when he was honest with himself, he had to admit he had no desire to go. With great trepidation, he approached his parents to ask if he could take some time off to work, save money, and start school the following year. Though it would have made sense for them financially, Sue reacted by saying, "Absolutely not! You are going to college in the fall." Carl had expected that response, but knew it was the wrong one for him personally. He was depleted and just not yet ready. In his first semester, he did so badly grade-wise that he was suspended for the spring term. From January through August, he worked in a grocery store and spent time with his parents, friends who were going to college locally, and people he met at this job. He also exercised, slept a lot, and read some books. By the time he returned to college eight months later, he felt ready. He did so well in the remaining semesters that he made the dean's list, got into a good graduate school, and went on to pursue a master's in geology. He plans to look for internships and then full-time employment with an environmental firm or governmental agency.

Sue had been afraid, like many parents, that taking a year off would mean that Carl would never ever get a degree. She worried that time away would mean he would lose momentum and be stuck working at a dead-end job for the rest of his life. However, in my experience, a purposeful and meaningful gap year, with a plan for attending college the following fall, has quite a different effect. The time off enables them to rest, engage with the world of work in some capacity, and to think about what is important to them and what they want to accomplish in college. That is why some schools are encouraging admitted students to take a year off.

A few years ago, Princeton University instituted the Bridge Program, through which admitted students could apply to participate in a community service program and defer enrolling for a full calendar year. Harvard's admission office "encourages admitted students to defer enrollment for one year to travel, pursue a special project or activity, work or spend time in another meaningful way."

Why would these elite colleges want high schoolers to wait? Because gap-year students really stand out on campus, in a great way. As a college administrator, I can tell from across the room which incoming first-years have taken time off. They are, first of all, the most well-rested. Most incoming students are shockingly over-wrought and sleep-deprived. They haven't had any time to slow down and think. Careening through life at high velocity significantly impairs their ability to know themselves, think clearly, and make good decisions, starting in the crucial first weeks of school.

Gap-year students are also strikingly more mature. They are not just one calendar year older. They have given thought over the past year to what they want to achieve, they have a more refined sense of purpose, and they can easily articulate it. That means they can let their advisors know how they intend to direct their energy while on campus, and the advisors, in turn, can give them the best advice to reach their goals. These students are usually far more capable of approaching faculty members without a lot of prompting and tend to establish productive relationships with more of them and make wiser academic choices. All of these factors contribute to a greatly enhanced academic experience.

Over the course of their college years, students who have taken a gap year also make better decisions about extracurricular activities, alcohol and other drugs, sex, and relationships. They have achieved some distance from the inevitable high school cliques and drama and begun to question the things that seemed so important in those years. Suddenly the crushes they had or the people they emulated fade into the distance. Give me two minutes with a brand-new freshman and I can tell whether they have come straight from high school or not. One year makes a big difference in energy, maturity, perspective, and focus.

Another advantage of a gap year spent working is that it will be a true plus in the minds of potential employers. Like it or not, as already mentioned, millennials are not beloved by many hiring managers. The children born between 1982 and 2004 have gained a reputation for being entitled, undisciplined, reluctant to roll up their sleeves and get their hands dirty, pathologically antagonistic toward constructive feedback, and just plain impossible to supervise. If your child has spent a year working somewhere—anywhere—it will be assumed that they have learned many lessons their peers haven't. Employers will reason that they will likely be more reliable, having practiced showing up and being accountable. They will not display loud disappointment when their paycheck isn't what they thought it would be, because they already understand what it means to pay for benefits and taxes. Their ability to get along with people who differ from them in every way will be enhanced. And a year working in the trenches speaks volumes not only about your child's work ethic but also about their individualism. They got off the unrelenting treadmill of high school to college and chose a different path than most of their peers. Any thoughtful manager in the work world knows that meant enduring a significant life adjustment and spending many hours alone at night when their friends were off at college, posting cheerful pictures on their favorite social media sites and boasting of their adventures.

Next Steps

If your child didn't get in anywhere, you have several great options.

- Consider calling a few admission offices to ask them if there were any red flags on the application.
- Many colleges have rolling admission, so there is still a good chance your child will be off to school in the fall. Take this as a real opportunity to explore some colleges you haven't discovered previously.
- A gap year is advantageous in many, many ways and should not be underestimated as a great option.

So, here you are. You've learned all you can, from as many sources as possible. The list of pros and cons is complete. You and your child have spent an enormous amount of energy and good thought on the decision about which college is the right choice and/or whether to wait a year to matriculate. Having considered the many sticky questions about cost and aid, the geographical areas, the range of academic offerings and support structures, the social and residential life on offer, and even the ways in which parent and family support are viewed, you are now more than ready to send in the deposit on May 1, if college lies ahead in the fall. It's been a rough but rewarding time for all of you. But armed with as much knowledge as you could get, you're ready to make the deposit. Congratulations, once again!

PART II

Four Months to Go: Staying Sane from May to August

How lucky I am to have something that makes saying goodbye so hard.

Now that the final decision is behind you, it's time to turn your attention to the months before move-in, which present new and, shall we say, interesting, challenges. These chapters will take you through all of the final steps to get your rising freshman to move-in day.

Just as important, it is time for you to begin thinking about what you are going to do after that watershed moment in *your* life. Indeed, as important as it is to help your child adjust to his or her new life away from home, these chapters will lead you through a brisk consideration of four broad areas of your life: your well-being in terms of your physical, mental, spiritual, and intellectual health; your professional and financial life; your social and community life; and, last but never least, your love and family relationships. But you will not be asked to take action yet! This period is for assessing where you are on each of these crucial dimensions, pondering roads not taken that might still be of interest, imagining and dreaming about possibilities, and taking steps to plan what you might undertake in the fall. Once you start giving some real thought to these aspects of your life, the creative juices will start flowing and you will probably surprise yourself with the breadth and depth of your ideas. Allowing yourself to dream—even if this is just the first of a number of children you will eventually send off on their own adventures—is but the first step toward realizing a new chapter of your life.

CHAPTER 3

The Dangers of Slumping Through Spring

College-bound seniors are usually so spent by the time they finish writing college applications and waiting for the life-determining acceptances and rejections that they stop paying attention to high school once the deposit has been sent to their future alma mater. Of course they are depleted. Of course they want to coast. Of course they need a break. But there are several reasons to keep going, and healthy ways to do it.

First, because college admission has become so competitive, institutions are paying ever closer attention to the final grades of each of their admitted students. I've seen too many students lose their spot in the freshman class because their grades decreased so significantly in the spring that the college revoked admission. Given how many people are competing for each available place, some admission offices can afford to be picky—they have long waiting lists of people eager to be moved to the admitted list. If your child slacks off enough in the spring, the college may decide they aren't as good a match for the school as they had once thought. An accepted student's academic record has to meet if not exceed the college's expectations from start to finish to keep that seat. After all that work, the applications, standardized exams, recommendations, and the emotional tidal waves of the process, no one wants to be in this situation. It is a nightmare for everyone involved, and especially for your child.

Behind the scenes, there are compelling operational reasons that motivate colleges to look closely at high school senior transcripts. Admission offices never know precisely how many students are going to apply. They also don't know what percentage of hopefuls will accept an offer of admission, the so-called yield, which they calculate by dividing the number of students who say yes by the number of offers they extend. It seems that they should know this, doesn't it? After all, they have historical data. But history is not as much of a guide as it once was. Students are applying to increasing numbers of schools every year, social media makes controlling the messages about a given school next to impossible, and the age of the Common App has made this trickier than ever. Sure, there are trends, but unexpected increases and decreases can spell disaster for overall college fiscal planning and health. The landscape is so unpredictable that we are seeing an unprecedented number of colleges merge with others or shut their doors altogether. It's a strange time in higher ed, and it promises to get even stranger in the coming decade.

Another important and seemingly odd variable in the college admission equation is the physical capacity of dorms and classrooms. If you get a bigger yield of students than you have space for, where will you house them? If a school guarantees housing, it may end up having to rent rooms in a local hotel. Another popular option, even among the elite schools, is to lease RVs or construct a trailer park on campus, as they are accessible, affordable, resource-light, and actually often far nicer than some of the dorms.

But finding housing for more people than anticipated is only the first problem. They then have to figure out where to put the additional classes that will be needed. A registrar's nightmare! Worse yet, who is going to teach them? Faculty plan their courses well in advance. Most schools require the fall lineup of classes by January or February, early enough in the spring semester for continuing students to register in March or April. Adding a course in July or August is a big no-no. Since faculty are already fully committed for the fall, departments have to turn to graduate students and adjuncts, who are asked at the last minute to learn new material and change their schedules to accommodate a new responsibility. It's a massive game of dominos. This is the reason the "enrollment managers," admission officers, course planners, department chairs, and advisors receive daily reports all summer long of the numbers of students who have "deposited," applied for housing, and registered for courses. Outsiders generally assume that college life is dead quiet in the summer, but in fact administrators and faculty are scrambling to plan based on the yield. So if a college has "over-yielded" its incoming class, it is highly motivated to find ways to reduce the size of the incoming class. Which is where the senior transcript comes in.

In a widely reported incident in 2017, UC Irvine revoked admission for 499 incoming students, ostensibly because their high school grades had dipped or they hadn't submitted their final high school transcript in time. As Vice Chancellor of Student Affairs Thomas A. Parham wrote: "Acceptance into all University of California campuses is provisional, contingent on meeting the contractual terms and conditions that were clearly outlined in your original admission offer. This includes submitting all academic materials such as transcripts and test scores by the agreed-upon deadline, upholding strong academic performance throughout the senior year of high school that meets agreed-upon thresholds, and having no discrepancies between the grades and courses you reported on your application and what we see once we review your official final transcript."

This was most likely a case of a college stringently enforcing the admission rules because they had over-yielded. By hundreds. Having no place to house or teach all the students they had accepted, UC

Irvine was well within its rights to rescind its offers for things that are usually considered a technicality. After enormous political pressure, the college reversed its revocation of admission for anyone whose transcript had not been submitted on time. I can only imagine the chaos on campus that August, trying to figure out how to accommodate several hundred extra students in dorms and classrooms.

What would you do if your child lost their place in the class they've imagined and committed to? After the shock wears off, you can consider three popular and productive options: (1) find a college that is still admitting incoming students in a second admission process or in rolling admission; (2) suggest your child sign up for classes at a local community college while thinking about how best to use this newfound time; or (3) plan a gap year from the get-go and reapply next year (see Chapter 2 for more on gap years). These aren't bad options, especially the gap year. But most students are frightened enough of the possibility of this happening that they can be encouraged to stay highly engaged in high school.

A second and related threat is the loss of scholarship monies if your child's final grades do not meet the threshold for receipt of funds. Nonprofits that grant these awards hope that the students they support will graduate, get good-paying jobs, and donate back to the organizations that made it possible for them to get a degree, thereby ensuring the financial viability of the organization. So it's important to them that they bet on the right students, so to speak. If your child doesn't make the grade at the last minute, they might renege on their gift and give it to the next deserving applicant. These organizations keep waiting lists for just this purpose.

A third reason to talk to your child about staying on top of things is that disengaging now will make it much more difficult to reengage when they get to campus. Let's say they are so drained and demoralized by the college application process and the inevitable changes looming before them that they decide in February that they need some time off from the craziness. They stop attending classes, or go to class and don't do much homework. They really just want to spend time with friends, or get in shape, or do absolutely nothing, and so they end up getting lower-than-usual grades. Even if they don't lose their spot in the matriculating class, by the time they arrive on campus in the fall, they will have taken over six months off from studying, quantitative and computational calculations, writing, and other academic practices. This means that they will be seriously out of practice for the rigors of college. After all, a half year is a very long period of time in the life of a seventeen- or eighteen-year-old. For them to hit the ground running when they get to their new campus would now be pretty unrealistic. Being out of shape academically is only going to add an unnecessary level of difficulty and stress to the transition. Explain to your high school senior that they are not just headed to a new school. They are headed to a new life. Habits of studying, reading, writing, attending class, doing homework—these are the baseline skills they need to succeed in the new environment, and they must be able to utilize them without thinking. They have to be rote habits of mind and action. At a minimum, college students must go to class, do homework, take tests, and write papers. They will have done themselves a disservice by disengaging in the routine academic activities over half a year before they need to use them in a focused way as they never have before.

This is what Taylor's family tried—and succeeded—in explaining to him. Taylor was the youngest of five brothers. The first four had gone to elite colleges in the Northeast, and he was expected to do the same. He was a math-science guy and wanted to pursue a degree in astrophysics with a minor in economics. When he got into Amherst College, he was thrilled. So were his parents. Now all five children would have degrees from great colleges. They would be set up for life, and the parents could stop the constant worrying that had become their routine. But once Taylor received the offer of admission, he stopped going to class and doing his homework. The family immediately noticed what was going on, so they all gathered on a Sunday evening for dinner and pounced on him. Each of the brothers told a story of either themselves or a friend giving up on academic work in senior year in high school or college (yes, it can happen again in four years!) and described the consequences. Tom's college roommate had had such a hard time getting it together in his freshman fall that he ended up with four C's. Brian himself had experienced a pretty spectacular senior slump in college, and his biochemistry grade had never recuperated, so he had had to apply to medical schools with a depressed science GPA, which still bothered him. He was convinced that he hadn't gotten into Harvard because of it. By the end of the dinner, Taylor was convinced. He would get his act together first thing the next day. He went to see each teacher, explained what had happened, and asked if he could make up the work he had missed. This could have been a catastrophe, but Taylor's family was able to bring him to his senses just in time.

Pre–Culture Shock

Slacking off is a common reaction to the concerted and protracted effort your child has put into getting to this moment in their lives. But there may be other things going on with them besides a need to rest or relax their standards at long last.

For starters, high school seniors preparing to go to college are keenly aware that their lives are about to change radically. I call this "pre–culture shock." It's the preparatory period leading up to change. They are moving out of the house. They have a palpable fear of losing their friends and know they are about to find themselves in unfamiliar social situations where they will have to make new ones. They are moving away from the family—and whether they think that is good or bad is immaterial. Having a new address is a big deal. They are leaving a known environment and going into the unknown, separating from teachers, guidance counselors, friends, extracurriculars, perhaps a religious community or a sports team, a community service role they have loved, and a predictable source of food and other sustenance. All of this is about to be visible only in the rearview mirror.

And they are going toward what? A lot of unknowns. Being about to face an untold number of mysteries can bring up all kinds of feelings and thoughts, from eager anticipation to anxious dread. Given the sheer number of songs and movies about "the good old days," nostalgic for the simpler days of high school or some other halcyon past, they know at least subconsciously if not consciously that they are about to go through something momentous. The real culture shock begins at move-in, but the pre–culture shock leading up to it can be just as debilitating. Consider a woman I'll call Susan. She noticed that her son Ryan seemed listless in the weeks since he'd decided where to go to college. When everyone else seemed to be celebrating their college admission, Ryan was withdrawing. Susan took him out to his favorite diner and asked him what he thought would change in the coming year, and was surprised when Ryan said he had two main fears. One was that his friendships with his three best friends would end in September. The other was that, not having applied to colleges as an athlete, he was terrified of not belonging to a sports team, which had been an important part of his days and identity since first grade.

These kinds of fears are legitimate and real. But there are a couple of relatively simple things that you, the parent, can do to help. The first and best remedy for exhaustion and a great cure for high levels of stress and anxiety is sleep. By now it is a commonplace that sleep deprivation is an epidemic in our country, especially among high school students. Figuring out ways for your kid to sleep a lot can be a family project involving scheduling mealtimes, reducing caffeine and sugar, eliminating unnecessary and, especially, stressful activities, creating quiet times in the household, and allowing teens to sleep until they awaken naturally whenever possible. Myriad studies outline as well the best ways to create "good sleep hygiene," which involves establishing regular sleep times, exposure to natural light during the day, avoiding stimulants and stimulation long before you hit the hay, comfortable beds and pillows, cleanliness, turning off all sources of light at bedtime, leaving the phone in the other room, and reducing noise during sleep hours.

A second productive way to counter pre–culture shock is to address it directly. That's what Susan did—she simply asked Ryan what *he* thought was going on, in a casual setting and a non-blaming way. She and Ryan then spent the rest of the meal thinking of how he could maintain his friendships in spite of the distance and looking up what sorts of teams he could join or club sports he could participate in at his new college.

Maybe your child will talk to you, a guidance counselor, or a therapist about the kinds of changes they anticipate in the coming months. Being able to articulate them helps to confront them and reduce the nervousness around them. In these conversations, encourage your child to identify the things that they hope will not change in the coming years in college, and then brainstorm ways for them to hold on to them. A significant portion of their anxiety is anticipating losses of all sorts, which can be incapacitating. Discovering and planning ways to retain the important things can be a powerful antidote.

Forms and More Forms! Responding to All Those College Communications

May is also the month when you and your child are bombarded with materials from the chosen college. They come by mail and email from a variety of different offices. A few colleges are quite organized about this; most are disastrously disorganized, with none of the internal offices that need things from you coordinating with one another. It's not unusual, for example, for Housing to have no clue what Health and Wellness, Disability Services, Advising, Billing, Financial Aid, Campus Engagement, and Orientation are sending you. The communications may not even look like they come from the same university. It is notoriously difficult for colleges to streamline, so what arrives in your virtual and real-life mailbox may feel like constant nagging. If it gets overwhelming, a helpful note of feedback to the Parent and Family Office letting them know about your experience is a good idea; it will give you an outlet for your annoyance, help them understand miscommunications and how they are coming across, and give them motivation for rethinking things for the next class. If there is no such office, then some version of the Marketing and Communications unit will likely do.

As annoying or overwhelming as all this correspondence may be, however, you don't want to throw any of it away in frustration; it's all extremely important. Your child will need to choose courses soon, but for now there are three important pieces of information you will want to prioritize: the housing application, pre-orientation information, and the orientation schedule.

The Housing Application and the Importance of Being Honest

Jennifer barely had time to think once she sent in her deposit. Her obligations to her sports teams, dance club, and volunteer position, in addition to homework and college applications, had left her stressed out. When the housing information arrived via email from her selected college, she gladly passed it on to her mother to deal with. Her mother quickly filled out the roommate preferences, among other requested info, and sent everything back the same day. When Jennifer and her roommate, Maida, moved into their room on the first day of orientation, they could not believe how different they were—and not in the educationally beneficial ways that colleges hope for. They had totally different sleep schedules, tidiness standards, noise level preferences, and music likes and dislikes. The list went on. Jennifer stormed into the dean's office a week into the term and demanded to know how such a mismatch could have been made.

The dean showed Jennifer the preferences sheets for both her and Maida and saw that they aligned perfectly. Jennifer remembered with a sinking feeling that she herself had not completed the form. She skulked out of the dean's office feeling rather ridiculous and not knowing how she was going to deal with the semester before her.

No one had malicious intentions here. Jennifer's mother filled out the form thinking that she was saving her daughter time and energy and securing an optimal match for her daughter. Because the mother and daughter had always considered themselves best friends, they could not have imagined that there would be a disconnect in their perceptions of Jennifer's preferences and the best possible roommate for her. For one, not only had the mother not realized how much organizing and cleaning she herself had done in Jennifer's room, but there had always been a housekeeper. Jennifer's natural tendency was to be unbelievably messy, something she knew about herself and had assumed her mother knew, too.

Living with a fundamentally incompatible roommate can be a recipe for disaster, especially when it could have been avoided. This cast a pall not just on Jennifer's and Maida's fall semester but on the entire academic year. When they asked repeatedly and stridently to move, they learned that shifting to a different room as freshmen would be next to impossible.

On the brighter side, students in this situation are sort of forced to hone their abilities to adapt, negotiate, and compromise. With the help of their RA, Jennifer and Maida eventually made peace with the situation and agreed on guidelines around sleep needs and a schedule of studying and socializing in the room. They also put a line of duct tape down the center of the room as a reminder to Jennifer of the boundaries of her mess. Additionally, they each got their own refrigerator because Jennifer's messy tendencies spilled over into food storage. These sorts of compromises are common, but the path to arriving at them is often rocky.

You, as the parent, are used to fixing or at least helping to fix your child's logistical issues, so you might be sorely tempted to get involved. Resist the urge! Unless your child's health and well-being are at risk, it is always best to encourage new students to try to work it out themselves and to suggest they turn to the many resources available at the university to settle disputes and aggravation. There are RAs and other support structures in the dorms, not to mention deans, advisors, ombudspersons, religious life staff, coaches, et cetera. The list of people willing to help is practically endless. Inevitably, if you do decide to call the college to make them aware of the situation, the RA will be alerted and help the roommates through a negotiation process.

Since most first-year students who live on campus will have to share a room, it is important to allow *your child* to fill out the questionnaires on lifestyle and to encourage them to respond *completely honestly*. It's best not to look over their shoulder as they complete it! Be sure to encourage your child to complete this paperwork thinking of how they want to live, not only how they have been living in your house so far.

Of course, many colleges are now allowing students to choose their own first-year roommate via social media. They may rely on Facebook or on one of the many companies that have popped up to help your child find the perfect rooming companion. Kids put tons of energy into this because they obviously want the first-year residential experience to be a good one, but more often than not they are making decisions based on superficial data. The likelihood of it working out is small. It's not the end of the world. They will survive, and they will use the first year to meet people they really want to live with in the coming years.

Why am I trying to get you not to worry about this? Because, as I have already hinted at, when it comes to trying to change rooms or roommates in your first year, the answer in most places is a firm no. Why? Because colleges are trying to fill every possible bed. They usually do not have extra rooms in their inventory in case roommates cannot work things out. They may have a few unassigned rooms designed for students with specific disabilities, since not all students complete the disabilities accommodations process before arriving, but once the college is informed, they must reasonably meet the needs. Keeping open beds to respond to roommate issues is just not financially feasible.

What most people do not realize is that the size of the incoming class in a college that requires first-year students to live on campus depends on the number of available beds. Some colleges raise enrollment numbers to increase their income and then have to triple students up in rooms designed for two people or even put two bunk beds in place of two single beds. They somehow manage to squeeze desks and closets into distressingly small spaces. This sort of housing arrangement doesn't bother some students; in fact, some embrace it as the "true college experience." Others, however, do not look forward to spending ten months in a tiny room with three strangers. And you might not appreciate that either, especially given the bill you are about to receive.

What makes the rooming situation even more difficult is that the overwhelming majority of college-bound students have had their own room or only had to share with one sibling at most. The thought of sharing with three people can be terrifying. But again, students do not have a choice unless they have a disability that requires a specific type of housing accommodation. So the best thing to do is to have them fill out the paperwork as honestly as possible, keep their minds open to whatever comes, and approach issues with grace, openness, and a sense of humor. After all, a disastrous roommate experience can become a humorous dinnertime story for years to come. Believe me, I know this from personal experience!

Mandatory Summer (and Orientation) Educational Programs

In order to ensure that students are prepared for college life, and in certain cases to comply with state and federal requirements, some colleges require students to go through summer training on sexual assault prevention; fire and personal safety; alcohol and other drug awareness; diversity, gender-based, and LGBTQA issues; among other things. If they don't do them in summer, you can be sure they will require students to attend them during orientation or shortly thereafter. Some of the initiatives are innovative; others are stale and old hat. Colleges try to make them as appealing as possible to incoming students so that they will attend, and some also use these as a bonding opportunity for the class.

Above all, these programs speak to the community's values and, more likely than not, to past legal or public relations issues the college and its lawyers have contended with. One college provides a poignant example of such a case. In the wake of the globally publicized sexual assault and defamation cases involving two undergraduates, the president of Columbia University created the Office of University Life, which, as its first step, developed a required educational program for all students, both undergraduates and graduate students, regarding sexual respect and community membership at the university. When your university hits the headlines for an incident like this, you can be sure that hundreds of hours are spent by dozens of people to figure out how to prevent it from happening again.

Since these topics have been receiving widespread attention nationwide, almost every college requires awareness-raising or training for students on the topics of sexual assault, domestic abuse, dating violence, stalking, and exploitation. Some are quite innovative, such as Rutgers's SCREAM (Students Challenging Realities and Educating Against Myths) Theater and SCREAM Athletes. The theater version of this program earned a mention in the White House's "Not Alone" document on bystander training, another recent requirement on many campuses. Bystander education teaches students how to help peers out of uncomfortable and even threatening interpersonal situations. Many schools are requiring their employees to complete educational modules about these topics as well.

Likewise, in the continuing wake of alcohol-related deaths on campuses, it is not surprising that many colleges require incoming students to complete online training on the use and abuse of alcohol and other drugs. AlcoholEdu for College is the most popular one. The rumor is that most students just click through it without paying attention to the content, which is a shame since the facts and figures contained there may surprise even adults. It does not take long to read the text, and most participants will learn something new and useful.

What's the Deal with *Pre*-orientation?

Many colleges offer pre-orientation—short programs that seemingly have nothing to do with college. Popular ones are outdoor experiences (hiking, biking, farming), cultural adventures (arts, music), and community engagement options focused on serving a local need (working in food pantries, building affordable shelter). These typically one-, two-, or three-day excursions are for incoming students and are usually led by older students. Though the pre-orientation leaders have been (in most cases) extensively trained, the idea of dropping your child off to head off into the wilderness for three days with people they have never met with not a single adult in sight may strike terror into your heart, or at least provide you with a few sleepless nights.

I have heard many parents say that they didn't allow their child to attend these because the schedule conflicted with a scheduled "final family vacation." They have been looking forward to this last bit of leisure time together before their lives change forever, they reason, and they want to hang on as long as possible and truly savor those last moments. Others explain that saying no is a kindness to their kids—so many new things await them, why add to it with a pre-orientation experience that takes them out of their comfort zone? A third big reason parents say no is, as mentioned, that some of these expeditions sound really scary. The college is going to send a herd of seventeen- and eighteen-year-olds off to a surprise destination to hike or bike and camp outdoors? The potential risks alone might make any logical human say no.

From the college's perspective, these jaunts achieve many goals at once. They provide a bonding experience that enhances the incoming students' sense of community, an opportunity to do something fun before the serious academic work begins, a way for freshmen to get to know peers and older students who lead the activities, a means of reducing the anxiety of starting college, and (much as it confirms some parents' worries about comfort zones) a very effective and productive way to get students out of their comfort zone. In other words, all that you might be worrying about is intentional: This abrupt break from everything known sets the tone for the unknowns of the whole college experience. Doing something totally different with completely new people helps students begin to explore new aspects of themselves, as they will continue to do throughout their time on campus. The leaders of these expeditions go through extensive training programs so that they are equipped to guide interactions among their charges and deal well with any eventuality that may arise. Colleges are nothing if not liability conscious, and you can be sure that their risk management folks have reviewed the trip plans with a fine-toothed comb before signing off on any plan that allows students to wield a hammer, trek in the mountains, or do food preparation. The pre-orientation leaders are also provided robust backup systems, so even the slightest hint of something going awry will activate a multi-layered and well-practiced response.

If your child's school offers one of these programs, my recommendation is to take them up on it. If you are concerned about finances, see if they offer financial aid for it. Most students find these trips extremely useful and fun—to begin understanding the culture of their new home, to allay fears, and to bond with other newcomers and therefore form a social network before arriving on campus. These can be very special experiences for everyone involved. Many students, in fact, stay in touch with their pre-orientation groups for years to come. If nothing else, it usually provides good memories and fun stories to tell.

Pre-orientation Notes

Look up your child's pre-orientation options and talk to them about participating. Though it's tempting to choose the one you are sure your child will excel at, if there are choices, think about which adventure might challenge them most. If your daughter is not much of an outdoor person, perhaps the hiking trip would be ideal. If your son doesn't know anything about sustainable farming, maybe that's the one for him. You get the idea. College is a time for them to test themselves in untold ways; this is just the first opportunity of many in the coming years.

Be sure to note the cost and the deadlines for responding and any equipment needed to participate. If your child has special needs, find the email address or phone number of the person in charge and call to ask if they can accommodate those needs. Do not try to hide special needs; trip leaders are only able to help if you let them know what is needed. If applicable, see if there is financial aid for the program and find the deadline for applying.

If your family has planned a final summer vacation that conflicts with the pre-orientation, you have a tough call to make. The time away is, after all, meant to mark this watershed moment in your collective lives. Should you keep the plan as is, or let your child join the pre-college adventure? Far be it from me to dictate the answer, but I can share with you that many, many students have expressed regrets to me in private that they weren't able to take advantage of this one-time experience. It might be best to let them attend while you luxuriate in your first vacation without kids! You might also consider a

family vacation later in the fall or at the end of your child's first semester. Check out the college calendar to see when your child might
have time off that aligns with your work or your other kids' schedules.

Looking Ahead

Find the college's incoming student orientation calendar. It can
have many names, like Calendar of Opening Days or simply New
Student Orientation Program. At this point, encourage your
child to print out the orientation calendar and the year's academic calendar and then go through both very carefully.

Important highlights of orientation:

- Is there a specific time period on that date when you should
  arrive?
- How long is orientation, and are there any mandatory
  events?
- What events are designed specifically for parents?
- What is your child expected to be doing at this time? (Often
  parents and students are separated for various reasons during orientation.)
- Is there an activities fair where students can peruse the various extracurricular options?
- Do they mount an academic fair where students can meet
  faculty, talk about courses and majors, and learn about research opportunities?
- When do classes start?

Why Colleges Require Orientation

By now, you are acutely aware of the move-in schedule. From that moment to the first day of classes is the incoming student orientation, a period of time every college spends months planning. In fact, highly organized schools start planning next fall's orientation very soon after this fall's classes begin! These days are carefully curated to give students the opportunity to settle into their new home in multiple ways. Freshmen meet residential and academic advisors, register for classes or adjust course schedules, ask lingering financial aid questions, meet other students, learn the terrain, get exposed to extracurricular options, learn the rules and responsibilities of being a community member, complete mandated educational programs (like sexual harassment discussions or anti-racism training), and organize themselves to begin classes.

Orientation also usually includes ceremonial events, like convocation, speeches by deans, receptions and dinners with alumni, and faculty talks. The opening days of a college are so important for students that reams of research exist on the best ways to mount the events that will help them transition to campus before they ever set foot in a lecture hall. That's why attendance is usually required. And even if it is optional, it is always best not to miss it. Not only does it offer a primer on a new vocabulary, landscape, friends, classes, and the overall culture of the place, but the ceremonies and talks given by faculty, administrators, and students can be meaningful and inspiring.

All colleges build some combination of social, co-curricular, extracurricular, and academic activities into this schedule. It is a great time for freshmen to start to get to know roommates, hallmates, residential advisors, academic advisors, and others who will serve as resources in the coming years.

If for some reason you suspect your child might not get to orientation on time, be sure to notify the college ASAP. On the day after move-in, administrators are combing through lists of the no-shows to figure out what happened. Is the student still planning to come? Or should they give the bed away to someone else? They have definitely already received roommate or dorm change requests. If something is standing in the way of your child attending orientation at all, the request to skip will probably be met with a resounding no. Colleges know that students who do not experience orientation miss a lot—rules, regulations, essential information, required training, bonding, and so on. Orientation days are planned months in advance and involve virtually every office on campus, and it is impossible to make up the experience afterward.

Managing Your Own Malaise: Your First Primer on Self-Care

You've helped your child stay engaged in their studies, responded to the college's many inquiries, and begun to plan the start of their year. All that busyness may have helped distract you from the sadness you might be feeling (or anticipating) about your child leaving home. And/or maybe this is the beginning of the celebration—you may be ready to let your kid go off into the world and be gleefully anticipating the newfound time for yourself. Either way, you've been busy and you've been thinking of everyone but yourself. Now it's time to turn to you.

Many parents have focused so exclusively on the changes their children are about to go through that they have dramatically neglected themselves. As the day of departure draws nearer, the stress might mount even more. Thinking about ways to prioritize your health will get you on the right path. Health can mean a lot of things; here, I am referring to everything from your physical and psychological state to your spiritual and intellectual well-being. You have certainly strived to provide your child with the best possible care in each of these areas. While you hope you have provided them with a solid foundation so that they can take it from here with some support from time to time, the most important thing you can do for yourself during this transition is to focus with love and care on your own needs.

This period is for assessing where you are on each of these crucial dimensions of your life and health, pondering roads not taken, imagining and dreaming about possibilities, and taking steps to plan what you might undertake in the fall in the wake of caring for one less (or any) child. Once you start giving some real thought to these aspects of your life, the creative juices will start flowing and you will surprise yourself with the breadth and depth of your ideas. In particular, allowing yourself to dream is but the first step toward realizing a new chapter of your life.

We begin, naturally, with your basic physical health. I know I don't have to convince you how important it is. But since you have been wrapped up in supporting your child through this journey, you may not have kept up with the fundamental necessities. This is the moment to begin remedying that. How long has it been since you've had updated immunizations, an annual physical, or age-related tests like a mammogram, PSA test, or colonoscopy? Are you due for a cleaning or X-rays at the dentist? All that might sound like torture, but if your doctors are anything like mine, you likely have to plan this far ahead to get appointments anyway. And you'll be glad to have them checked off your list early in the fall.

Beyond these healthcare basics, are there lifestyle changes you want to try to make? Have you been meaning (for years) to lose weight or quit smoking? Have you wanted to finally take up yoga or meditation or simply redeem that Groupon for a free makeup consultation? Some people take enormous pleasure in undertaking a new food regimen when they no longer have to feed children or the picky one who is now being fed on campus. Others take this opportunity to rekindle a love of an old sport or to start a completely new physical activity. Do you miss swimming? Do you want to take up golf? Or is hang gliding more your thing? One mother I know committed in May to making September her moment to take up running again. She hadn't run since her twenties, so she started with an app and ran her first marathon before the end of her son's freshman year. The father of one rising freshman used his son's senior spring semester to start recruiting members of a birding group—he liked the idea of a long walk with friends once a week come fall. Putting yourself in motion will not only make you healthier physically but also stimulate your mind and help you center yourself in the upcoming transition.

While planning to focus on your physical self will certainly improve your psychological outlook, it may also be time to think about your mental well-being. Especially during periods of change, attention paid to our state of mind helps us weather it well. The goal is to be mindful of the enormousness of the shifts taking place in our lives and to make good decisions. After all, your very self-identity is undergoing a redefinition. You are moving from being a full-time parent to being the parent of an adult child. If you have raised an independent child whose attachment to you is healthy, then they will need you with ever-decreasing frequency. They will include you less often in their daily lives. Now you are faced with the question of how and how easily you will detach from their constant physical presence in your life and how to redirect your energies.

This is also a good time to consider psychological goals, too. Are there behaviors or patterns of action and thought you would like to amend? Do you think frequently about something about yourself that annoys you or makes it hard to function at the level you would like? Are you dependent on someone you would prefer to be independent of? I live in New York City, where we don't ask *if* you are in therapy; we ask *what day* you see your therapist. Being in an environment that so destigmatizes help-seeking is unusual, I realize. But, as I always say to undergraduates, seeking help is a sign not of weakness but of strength. Knowing how and when to look for support is a true indicator of maturity and wisdom. If you, as an adult, know when to reach out for some assistance in the way you lead your life, you will also be modeling that essential tool for your child who will need to do the same on their campus and throughout their lives.

Part of psychological health is bound up with our physical environment. Maybe you've been fantasizing about scrubbing down your child's now-empty room or turning it into something for yourself. (Caution on that one—quick changes might rattle your kids, so if you have a plan in mind, be sure to share it with them first!) Stop for a moment and consider how your home, your office, and any other spaces where you spend time make you feel. Are they a true reflection of who you are and what you value? If not, what needs to change? How about scheduling some time to clear the desk, files, and shelves of unneeded and unwanted stuff? What about digging through your closets and donating what you haven't worn in years to a worthy cause? Cleaning out might do you a world of good. It clears your mind, energizes you, and jump-starts a process of making real, positive change. But again, at this time, all you are doing is imagining and scheduling. No action is needed. Just start considering whether there are elements of your home that could use some attention so that it affords you more comfort, enjoyment, and even delight. One parent I worked with tackled her home immediately upon returning from the college drop-off. She kind of dreaded the process but told me later that it was both fun and liberating. And at the end of it all, she had mountains of items to give to friends and relatives and to donate to a deserving community organization, which added to her sense of well-being. Even though she had an inkling that this would provide her with some relief, she couldn't believe the elation she felt at every turn. It was as if she was making a physical statement of the beginning of a new life. She was thrilled. It may seem strange to emphasize this, but our home, however small or large, is our haven and should provide us with maximum physical and psychological comfort and, yes, even joy.

Don't Forget Your Spiritual Self

Before you were a busy, carpooling, and application-deadline-nagging parent, you were likely more in touch with your spiritual self, the invisible parts of yourself that drive your insights, thoughts, and actions. Or maybe you never were. Either way, now's your opportunity!

Some people find their way to this part of themselves through involvement in organized religions, and others do it on their own through formal or informal practices. Whatever your method, introducing or reintroducing a means to finding your way to yourself on a regular basis can help you eliminate negativity and increase well-being and happiness.

You do not have to have disposable income to do this. There are many cost-free ways to find quietude and center ourselves. The return on your investment can be high. Get back into the habit of attending a weekly religious service, learn to meditate by using an app, read poetry, visit a museum, or start the habit of a daily solo walk.

Finally, let's turn to your intellectual well-being. Once you no longer have to think so much about your child's daily needs and preparing them for the world of college and career (even if you have another approaching the same college acceptance gauntlet, it'll be a little easier this time around given your gained experience), you will have room for new thoughts and ideas. What better time is there to dive into an unfamiliar subject or a different author's works, or even to begin *writing* poetry, prose, or a blog—or maybe creating a vlog? Have you been meaning to start a book club or learn a new language? Catch up on a list of award-winning movies you never got to see? What about auditing a class at the local college or continuing education center (note: *not* a class at your child's new school)? Bottom line: Planning to invest more deeply in the many aspects of your well-being not only will help you transition to a new phase of your life but also will send a powerful signal to your child, who will be exploring a new chapter of their own life.

Summer Musings

This is the time for you to start directing your energies toward yourself.

- Thinking about what you need and want with respect to your health is a productive and energizing first step.
- Consider ways to engage in physical, mental, spiritual, and intellectual practices once your child goes off to school.
- There are infinite possibilities. Imagine all that you will be able to do in the fall!

CHAPTER 4

Summertime Strategies

June is a hectic month for the high school senior and the family. There are finals to take and recover from and celebrations to plan and attend. Once that is all behind you, there is a certain July-August nervousness that comes from seeing something concretely coming to an end with an unknown beginning looming. This is the ideal period of time for everyone to confront and discuss the absence of a surefire recipe for realizing post-college dreams. I call this the "formula-for-life problem." By understanding the lack of a direct correlation between majors and careers, you will be able to suggest practical ways for your rising freshman to think about academic and professional choices expansively, realistically, and productively as they get ready to register for fall classes as early as June or July.

These are also the months for you to begin to imagine what you would like to undertake with respect to your professional life and fiscal health in the fall. With this child off to college, you may have more time and energy to spend reinvigorating your career or other engagement in the world outside of your home. And with the tuition and fees coming due, you will want to take a renewed look at your family's overall financial situation and make plans toward enhancing it.

The Formula-for-Life Problem

High schoolers have been hearing for years from parents, teachers, guidance counselors, and peers that the courses they take, the extracurriculars they participate in and lead, the volunteer experiences they choose, the standardized test scores they get, and the grades they earn will all add up to admission to a given range of colleges. In other words, so far, life has gone along with some version of this pretty reliable formula in mind.

Courses + Extracurriculars + Volunteer work + Standardized test scores + Grades = Several colleges to choose from

The formula has proven its mettle; after all, following it to their best ability has gained them college admission. Why wouldn't there be a similar way to approach college to get to the next goals in life? When students start signing up for fall classes, it is natural for them to assume they will get a similarly dependable way to get the golden ring. In fact, quite naturally, students (ever more frequently with their parents in tow) often get to their first advising appointment expecting to be told what it is. I always hated being the person to tell a new student that the next four years would be relatively formula-less. I wasn't going to be able to tell them which courses to take, much less which minors and majors to choose, because there are few predetermined plans for success. They were going to have to do it themselves by following their hearts and minds. Not only that, but their major might not have anything to do with their future career whatsoever. Some people get angry and think I'm an idiot, not doing my job, or hiding something. Others are disappointed or scared. Still others are overjoyed when they learn that there are very few concrete formulae that might resemble this:

Courses + Extracurriculars + Major + Minor + Civic engagement + Internships + GPA = Careers A, B, & C

The lack of a surefire formula in college is probably one of the biggest stumbling blocks to success, because believing that there is one narrows possibilities and denies students the chance to approach the curriculum as if it were a fantastic smorgasbord. For there is no real recipe for degree completion beyond this:

Go to class + Do homework + Study + Take exams + Ask for help when you need it + Fulfill degree requirements = College degree

If students would embrace this as a truism from the moment they left high school, college life would be much easier. But it is a difficult shift to make. Because what this means is that all of the decision-making is up to them. Even if they plan to become a doctor, lawyer, or businessperson, the major and minor are still quite open. You do not have to major in a science to go to medical school. (About half of incoming medical school students have majored in something non-science-related.) You do not have to choose political science or history to go to law school. (Law schools, like medical schools, love to admit an intellectually diverse cohort every year. And law schools are getting less and less picky given that the numbers of applications have plummeted in the past few years.) And if you want to be a successful businessperson, you do not have to major in economics. (In fact, one of the Sachs of Goldman Sachs once told me that 85 percent of their new employees needed no more than macro- and microeconomics. Furthermore, they appreciated a task force of people who had vastly different specialties, as it brought depth and multiple perspectives to every team.) As a parent, you can do your child a favor and disabuse yourself of these notions immediately. Your child can engage in any extracurriculars that interest them. They can do lots of volunteer work. They can apply for internships in myriad areas of potential interest. And they can study in countries around the globe. It is all up to them from now on—with your help and the college's, of course.

There are four notable exceptions to this point: careers in engineering, the sciences, mathematics, and academia. Engineering curricula are strictly regulated by a central accrediting body, called ABET. Science majors have a large number of prerequisites, which must be started in year one if they hope to advance in the field. The road to completing the basic coursework in general and organic chemistry, physics, calculus, and biology is typically laid out very clearly in any college catalog. Mathematicians start early as well. They usually know who they are and find a home very quickly in the math department, where professors take them under their wing immediately. After all, a good undergraduate mathematician is a true rarity and worth their weight in gold. And if a life in the ivory tower is the goal, a solid undergraduate experience in the area of interest is an absolute necessity. So if your child is planning to be an engineer, scientist, mathematician, or Ph.D.-holding professor, they will need to pay close attention to the relevant course sequences from the get-go.

Beyond those, there are not many fields that require that sort of academic planning. That means students are going to have a vast number of choices before them. The best tool for winnowing down interests is, in fact, the college catalog. First of all, it contains a list of academic programs. That means the degrees, majors, minors, certificates, and other options for acquiring credentials there. Colleges vary widely in their offerings and even somewhat in the names they give to various areas of study.

When high schoolers peruse the catalog, they may have to admit that they don't know what some of these fields even are. The offerings are so rich! Understanding the options up front will aid the decision-making process in the coming years. The beauty of it all is that every final transcript relates a story of a unique person's path on the intellectual throughways of college.

Why am I going on and on about this here? Because many colleges now advise and register incoming students in summer, well before they set foot on campus. Before the first advising appointment, whether it is a group presentation or a one-on-one appointment, your child will want to be aware of academic options and the elasticity of the relationship between a major and their lives beyond college.

And, obviously, there are not just going to be academic choices to make. Extracurriculars of all sorts beckon new students. Perhaps they have always wanted to learn how to take great photographs or do layout for a student newspaper or magazine. Or maybe rowing is appealing, so they are thinking of trying out for the crew team. Extracurriculars will have an enormous impact on the development of your child's passions, connections, and careers. Whether or not these activities are on the transcript (some colleges have adopted the experiential transcript to include out-of-classroom learning), they will indeed find a prominent place on a résumé and provide conversation starters in interviews down the road.

Why am I so insistent on disabusing you of the notion that your child needs to adhere to a magic formula in college to succeed? Because statistics show that current college graduates are going to change their careers multiple times in their lifetimes. Rare is the person in the twenty-first century who will graduate from college, enter a career, and stay there for the next four or five decades. Today's students are preparing themselves for unknown futures. A recent report by Workday on the future of work notes: "What will separate the top talent from everyone else in the workplace of tomorrow will be a flexible and growth mindset that recognizes learning never ends." That article and scads of others highlight the importance of competencies and skills learned in and out of the classroom as the means to securing future employment. What these articles don't do is list required coursework or activities. Because the ideal employee is not one who necessarily has specific facts in their head; it's someone who has the skills and competencies coveted in today's world of work. Again, unless they plan to be an engineer, enter a scientific or mathematical field of some sort, or be a college professor, there may be little to no direct correlation between the field they major in as an undergraduate and their many future professions.

So, how should they go about making decisions? This can be a very unsettling situation. If they are used to relying on the formula they followed in high school, the absence of such a surefire recipe for college and post-college life can be anxiety-provoking. Given that the major does not play a necessarily determinative role in one's career, how else do you go about figuring out what to pursue? That same report says, "The problem for higher education to solve . . . is that students often come to campuses focused on finding a major that will lead to a job." But the jobs they need to prepare for may not yet exist. (This is but one example of the ways in which the academy hasn't caught up to the world around it.) Nevertheless, unless the college does not require a major (there are famously few in this category), a decision has to be made at some point. Yes, it seems eons down the road, but your choices narrow quickly after the first year, since so many majors have prerequisites that have to be successfully completed in the first four semesters. It's a conundrum. On the one hand, a major probably won't determine your child's future career. On the other, students have to prepare to commit to one in two or three or four semesters, and prereqs have to be done by then. It may seem overly type-A advice, but I am utterly convinced that incoming students do themselves a great service by getting the lay of the land in the summer before arriving.

Majors, Minors, and Certificates Galore

The first step to making the best choice is to know what the majors are and how the college defines them. A major typically lives in an academic department. The college funds each of these, and some receive significant monies from outside sources as well, which can mean funded summer research and travel for undergraduates and graduate students alike. Departments are the organizing principle of the college's faculty, administrators, scholarship, and academic offerings. Some universities also have centers and institutes (discussed in Chapter 2), which are separate entities that may or may not offer courses and majors/minors to undergrads. Using the list of academic departments and institutes that offer undergraduate programs, majors, and minors at their future college, your child can do one exercise in particular that will help clarify potential directions at this point.

Every college has a finite number of academic offerings. (Many have as well an option of creating your own major, but I do not generally recommend that, for reasons explained below.) Every entering college student should be familiar with the majors on offer and be able to describe each field of study in general terms. I have done the following simple exercise with dozens of college students, and every single one—future majors in astrophysics, linguistics, comparative literature, and poetry—has found it illuminating in their decision-making processes, not just at the beginning but over the course of several semesters.

- With your new high school graduate, get out a piece of paper and pen or start a new document on a computer and make three columns: "Definitely (+)," "Maybe (?)," and "Definitely Not (X)."
- Then work your way together through the college catalog, reading the first few lines describing each major and minor. As you read the entry for history, if you notice your kid's eyes glazing over and some yawning, that major should go into the "Definitely Not" column. If they start reading about computer science and want to know more, but are not completely sure about it, put it in the "Maybe" column. And finally, if they read the de-

scription of mathematics and find it absolutely scintillating, put that in the "Definitely" column. Once every major and minor finds a place in a column, they can use this list to guide course choices for the upcoming semester. You may even be surprised to see some interesting patterns developing in the columns.

- Taking the now-finite list in the "Definitely" column, your child is ready to look over the introductory courses in each of those fields to start constructing a course lineup for the first year. If they have room, they may even be able to check out a course in the "Maybe" column.

I encourage students to bring this document to the first advising appointment and then refine the columns over time, leading up to major declaration. Some open it every semester when choosing the next semester's courses. Though the exercise is simple, every single student has reported to me that it helped shape their thinking about choice of course, major, minor, and even internships and extracurriculars. Its power lies in revealing both expected and unexpected fields of interest, making future decisions that much easier. It has the added advantage of making you and your child familiar with all of the majors and minors offered. As already stated, some colleges have no majors. Some don't encourage or permit minors, and some call them something else altogether (e.g., concentrations). Some even call majors concentrations. The presence or absence of some areas of study can be quite determinative. If your child has done this exercise, they will already be ahead of the game.

As your child plays with the potential fall schedule, it may be helpful to know if students can freely add and drop courses in the first week or two. Some schools refer to this as "shopping period" (a term most faculty can't stand, by the way). The free add/drop period gives students the chance to visit lots of classes, pick up syllabi, hear the instructor describe the course and the required work, and get a real sense of whether it's a fit or not. I think it's invaluable. Of course, there may be courses that can't be changed at all. An advisor will tell you all you need to know in this regard. The registrar's site will list the add/drop deadlines, too.

The major is but one of the things they are going to choose at some point. The extracurriculars, as mentioned, are going to be just as important. Why? Because students leave college with a wide range of skills, some of which are developed in the classroom, but many of which are also (or only) honed in out-of-classroom activities. In fact, when they begin to submit résumés for internships and jobs, they will find that many interviewers will be especially interested in their extracurricular engagements because it is there that young people hone the skills and develop the competencies that are most valuable to employers.

Two Handy Tools for Making the Tough Decisions

When students are perplexed or overwhelmed by the choices, two organizations come in very handy.

1. NACE (National Association of Colleges and Employers) has developed competencies that college students need for the world of work. You can think of it as a resource for translating what is learned in college to the practical necessities of future careers.
2. Burning Glass Technologies has identified eight skills that undergraduates should hone to double their job prospects.

See the Additional Resources section for contact information.

Virtually any standard college experience will ensure that a student is employable by the time they graduate. Keeping in mind that "companies and organizations are looking for a set of diverse competencies that no one academic major provides," as the Workday report notes, it will be your child's job to interpret what they learn on campus and find ways to include it on the résumé. Any college should have career services professionals to help with that.

What we are talking about here is what colleges refer to as some version of "major choice initiatives" or "translating majors to careers." Because so many students flock to majors they have heard of in high school or the ones they believe will land them the best job opportunities, like economics, political science, and psychology, college administrators are obsessed with designing campaigns that will encourage students to choose the lesser-known fields of study. To do this, they offer examples of alumni who have majored in, say, German, philosophy, or sociology and gone on to great success in finance or entrepreneurial ventures or great fame in some unexpected arena of life.

Wellesley College's website offers an impressive infographic showing the range of possible trajectories from each major, with an interactive visualization of alumnae majors and their eventual careers. It represents data on real people. Plus, it illustrates pointedly that just about any major can lead to just about any career. Armed with this idea, that majors and careers are not aligned as neatly as we might want, you should feel free to encourage your child to explore courses and fields widely. We fetishize the major in spite of it making little or no difference in our eventual career opportunities in the majority of cases. What students really need to focus on is what they love and how the knowledge they gain and the skills they hone relate to the world of work.

A case in point: Elisa came from humble means. She knew that her high school had not prepared her for what she imagined was going to be a very rigorous freshman year, so was happy to take part in a summer program prior to her first year that was designed for kids like her. She took two courses that summer, English and sociology. She had no idea what sociology was, but when it turned out to be the study of human societies and relational interactions, she became fascinated. "But what could I *do* with a major in sociology?" she asked her advisor, who responded, "Anything you want." Elisa thought he was oversimplifying it at best or daft at worst. Noting Elisa's skepticism, he showed her the NACE competencies. He also cited multiple examples of alumni who had studied sociology and gone on to medical, law, or graduate school in pursuit of a Ph.D. and careers in finance, art gallery management, and higher education. One had gotten a Fulbright to study in Korea; and another had taught English in Singapore for three years before returning to the United States to join the Foreign Service. Elisa was surprised when he then spent a lot of time talking with her about her extracurricular interests. Before she left, he asked her to bring a rough draft of her résumé next time. The following week, he spent another hour with her poring over the skills and competencies she had developed in high school and could potentially hone in out-of-classroom activities on her new campus. She was astonished to learn that relevant skills from her leadership positions in secondary school organizations could add so much to her résumé. She began thinking about her activities in terms of what she had learned might pique an employer's interest. Looking back on her past, she realized she had learned project management, negotiation, presentation skills, work ethic, professionalism, and teamwork in Model UN. She had also acquired the skills of negotiation, time management, applied learning, and resourceful creativity as a babysitter for her neighbors. Third, she was now convinced that she wanted to join a campus club sport to hone her collaboration and teamwork skills, knowing that employers would see discipline, focus, persistence, and stamina in people who commit themselves to structured physical and endurance participation.

I love to cite the example of a Harvard alumnus—we'll call him Doug—who went on to become a self-made billionaire. Whenever he spoke to undergraduates, they asked him what he majored in, and they were shocked when he said, "Philosophy." They'd expected him to say economics. He would respond to this inevitable reaction by explaining that studying philosophical thought was the single most important thing he had done while an undergraduate, as it prepared him for the world of business like nothing else could have. In fact, he attributed his extraordinary financial success to his understanding of human nature, which he gleaned through his study of the pillars of Western and Eastern philosophies. The courses had forced him to wrestle with philosophical problems of the ages. This alum experienced success not only in the business world but also in the political realm, in philanthropic endeavors, and in his personal life. When he was an undergraduate, the philosophy department had welcomed him and made him feel that he belonged. He got to know professors and graduate students, and truly enjoyed the intellectual and social opportunities there. It became an academic home to him. There are thousands of people like Doug who illustrate that there is no obvious formula for the life your child is about to create.

Another touchpoint in this discussion is the list of job titles that firms are actively recruiting for that did not exist ten, twenty, or thirty years ago. When you were a teenager, could you have anticipated that companies would now need wind farm supervisors, app developers, drone operators, sustainability managers, or chief mindfulness officers? The organizations that need these positions are looking to people with translatable skills and experience, not someone whose college major matches the job description. Especially in this so-called age of disruption, innovation, technology, and entrepreneurship, the name of the game lies in ever-accelerating change. It is exciting to imagine what kinds of new work will be available to your child when they graduate!

By the way, every college boasts superb career services or career education offices, but you will find that many if not most of them are sadly understaffed. They may serve many and varied student populations and interests, and they have to organize workshops on networking, résumé-building, and job-seeking strategies; hold job fairs that involve dozens if not hundreds of employers; offer mock interviews; establish and maintain relationships with employers; look for internships both in the United States and abroad; deal with crises; keep abreast of the ever-changing world of work; engage in professional development; understand global employment trends; and respond to student and parent inquiries. It can be hard to get an appointment and even impossible to see the same career counselor twice. Many of these offices have to resort to "express advising" models because they simply do not have the resources to give each student the sort of in-depth attention they may want and need. Not all is lost, though. While one-on-one attention can be hard to get, group venues can be effective. One is the career services workshop, which will focus on topics from résumé writing and interview skills to self-branding and social media dos and don'ts. Students who actively engage in these starting from the first year benefit a great deal.

Some schools discourage freshmen from utilizing the career office at all. The college may not have the capacity, or they might say they believe that it is healthier to focus only on academics at first and not on the career. I think that is unrealistic and just plain bad advice these days. Preparing for the world of work begins on day one. Academics who want to deny that students need to attend to the necessary practicalities of life after college have been accused of everything from elitism to ostrichism. The bottom line is that our society has changed a lot in the past few decades, and ignoring post-college obligations to one's family, community, and the planet is a luxury few can afford.

How to Help Your Child Start Engaging with Career Counselors

Check out the career services website of your child's college.

- How many career counselors are there? Are they the same as academic advisors, or is there a separate office?

- If it is a university, are the career services staff members serving students in the liberal arts and in the professional schools? Undergraduates and graduate students?
- How many counselors are available just for undergraduates?
- Where is the office located?
- How do students make an appointment?
- How many career fairs do they have every year? In which industries?
- What is the schedule of workshops?
- Do they list the staff members' names and contact information?
- Do they serve alumni or only current students?

Knowing ahead of time what resources are available in this area will ensure that you set your expectations appropriately and, more important, can steer your new college student well.

The name of the office designated to help with careers can be telling. Is it Career Services, Career Development, Career Education, or Career Strategies, for example? It takes untold hours for schools to agree on the moniker that reflects their intention. One thing for sure is that they are decidedly not job placement offices. They are not going to find your son or daughter a job. But they will help them think about their imagined futures, lead them to articulate the goals that are most in alignment with their stated and ever-evolving needs and desires, and teach them how to express those goals in résumés, interviews, and networking encounters. In other words, they help students develop the tools that give them the best chance of securing a job. These offices provide the resources students need to educate themselves on the best ways to establish and pursue a career, and some will offer fruitful opportunities for interaction with employers. The names Career Development and Career Education reflect a deliberate rejection of the idea of job placement. The staff will work hard to expose students to good industries and employers, but the work of securing a position needs to be done by the students.

Top-notch college career services should also be able to connect students with alumni in any number of professions. Since over 80 percent of jobs in the United States are obtained through personal connections, and an equal percentage of openings are never advertised publicly, lurking in the so-called hidden job market, seeking out a college's alumni may be the most productive thing students can do for their future careers.

The Pros and Cons of an Independent Major

This brings me to the point about independent majors. Many students arrive on liberal arts college campuses certain that they will pursue a major of their own design, so they don't pay any attention at all to the majors and minors. Sure, it sounds appealing, exciting, and bold. But most of the majors they have in mind will fall into an already existing department. Plus, the experience of belonging to an academic home cannot be underestimated. Just as it was for Doug, the department is the place where faculty, graduate students, and undergraduates interact to form a community interested in a particular mode of inquiry. It may mount seminars for majors, have a lounge for relaxing and studying, or offer a kitchen as a gathering place. They might invite undergraduates to teas, talks by guest faculty, and a host of other intellectual and social opportunities only for people connected to it. Pursuing an independent major means missing out on what can be an extremely edifying, comforting, and engaging academic and social experience.

Academic departments are worlds unto themselves, with a budgetary and administrative structure, a chairperson, committees, faculty, staff, and facilities. They can be so all-encompassing that many faculty and graduate students spend all of their time there and do not venture out to other departments very often, if at all. Since departments offer talks, conferences, films, lunches, and dozens of other ways of gathering the community together, it is possible that students won't need to look elsewhere for interaction and collegiality once they declare a major or even before. Any undergraduate who is invited to a departmental function should rearrange their schedule to go. These can be enriching and fun events and a great way to get to know the field and the people who have dedicated their lives to it. I've known lots of students who gave up some of their extracurricular activities, like a sport, fraternity, sorority, or dance troupe, so that they had more time to spend in the academic home that had embraced them.

Sometimes an independent major just cannot be avoided. This is particularly true when a student wants to pursue a cutting-edge field of study that does not yet have a department. Quantitative neuroscience, cognitive science, digital humanities, and intelligent systems are examples of emerging fields that some universities have not yet had the chance to fund and recruit faculty for. If your child's interests lie in such a field, you will want to check out the process that students follow to apply for their own major. The proposal will likely require the submission of recommendation letters from faculty who will advise them, so it is imperative that the college have people who are already at least peripherally engaged in the study of the relevant topics. Even when asked, many faculty will decline the request to guide an independent major, not because they are not interested but because they just don't have time. Taking on one independent major who will inevitably require a lot of additional energy is not always manageable.

Taking the Anxiety Down a Notch

When anxiety starts to get the better of you or your child, remember:

- There is no surefire formula for preparing for the rest of life. The path your child paves will be unique and should be an organic outgrowth of their own needs, obligations, and desires for the future.
- College students should explore widely, both academically and extracurricularly. They will gain useful and translatable skills and knowledge in every endeavor.
- There is not necessarily a particular major one should choose in order to be qualified for a particular job out of college (unless they want to be an engineer, scientist, mathematician, or college professor).
- Most majors can lead to an infinite number of careers.
- Some of your child's future professions and job titles may not exist yet.
- Every college curriculum should prepare students well for the world of work.
- Career services professionals will help students translate what they learn in high school and college into a résumé that will appeal to employers of most any stripe.
- It will be your child's job to make sure future employers can readily see what makes them and their skills and competencies appealing as candidates.

You may think I've gone on about this quite enough or too much. But the number of students and parents who have misconceptions about majors is staggering. Before your child registers for fall courses this summer or when they arrive on campus, depending on the school, spend some time questioning your own assumptions so they can begin to question theirs. It will help your child think expansively and creatively about their pursuits in the coming four years. Also, the vast majority of incoming freshmen are pretty underprepared for the initial advising meeting that takes place before registration. That's a waste of everyone's time and energy. Some haven't taken a look at the freshman requirements or know the number of credits they need in order to be considered full-time students. Still more imagine that the college course lineup mirrors high school's, so they think they will naturally take some sort of English or literature course, math, history, a science, and a language. This is almost never the case. And it is not uncommon for people to believe that the only major that prepares you for law school is political science or history, that premed students have to major in science, or those who aspire to financial careers must major in econ. You get the picture.

Time to Focus on Your Own Future, Again!

Indeed, our world of work and our economic security are two important sources of both our identity and well-being. They are usually, though not always, intertwined. Regardless, parents often put off changes to their professional domain until they don't need to take care of children so much anymore. It stands to reason, since time, energy, and focus can be short when you are raising kids. If you are like millions of others, you will take the opportunity of your only child or at least this one heading off to college to take stock of what you have accomplished so far and what more you want to do. Even if you still have one or more children at home, the departure of each one can be that wonderful moment when you may start to see light on the horizon. There's no time like now to start imagining the possibilities. You can finally invest more energy into your career, and pay more attention to your finances. And since having a child in college puts a strain on the budgets of so many, diving more enthusiastically into your work might be a must. The more purposeful you are when you consider your needs and desires, the more able you will be to plunge headfirst into executing plans when the fall rolls around. So this summer, find some moments to reflect on your career, your profession, your world of work, whatever you prefer to call it, and the degree of your engagement in it. Then you'll be ready to take action in September.

Focusing on You

- Do you spring out of bed in the morning looking forward to your daily work? Is it satisfying? Are you engaged? Do you yearn for a change?
- How is your work-life balance? Do you want to work more or less? Do you want more or less "you time"?
- Would you like to make new and different connections, join different organizations, and/or attend conferences?
- Is it time for you to seek a promotion? Change careers? Write a book? Write a paper?
- As you think back, do your roles align with what's now most important to you?
- What were your professional moments of the highest energy and excitement?
- When did you experience the deepest calm, comfort, and contentment in your career?
- Are there paths you might have taken that are still open to you? Have potential new directions occurred to you in the past ten or twenty years?
- Are you at a crossroads that requires some decision-making?
- Will the fall be a good time for you to make some changes?

This is a perfect moment for you to renew your childlike curiosity and wonder so that you enter this time of ambiguity in a constructive, holistic, and open-minded way. What's even more important is to approach this with a nonjudgmental stance toward yourself, your dreams, and your aspirations. You will be in new territory, with few signposts and infinite possibilities. Give yourself the freedom to use your imagination!

When Joel and Sam's second and younger child left for college, they anticipated that "empty-nest feeling," and they had no idea what they were going to do with themselves. Joel knew he had to throw himself into his psychoanalytic practice to increase his income now that they had two kids in college at the same time. In spite of the enormous financial pressure, he now found a few minutes a week to write. After all, he had a drawerful of the beginnings of things from years ago. He also began guitar lessons after teaching himself for years. And finally, he spent more time engaged in small political acts, such as petitioning, calling congresspeople, and participating in demonstrations. Sam, for her part, had already begun something completely new when their first child left for college—teaching a childhood education course at a community college, which she found more demanding and involved than she could ever have imagined.

In other words, you don't have to wait until all the stars align—for your kids to graduate from college and your financial life to be stable again—to think about the future. One of the most powerful tools you can use to explore potential choices of career and life in general is "informational interviewing," and you can start it anytime. Why not start setting some up now, in summer, for the fall?

In case you haven't done it before, informational interviewing is a short conversation between you and someone who is engaged in an area and/or organization that holds some interest for you where they describe what their professional world is like, how they got there, how gratifying it is, and what they like and don't like. When I suggest doing these, most people look at me as if I've grown another head.

Maybe they remember the informational interview process that often precedes a first job out of college—it's a good practice then as well, of course. But it is economical in terms of cash and time as well as enormously educational and inspirational to do this again now, as an adult looking toward a new chapter.

There's nothing like meeting people who have experience in a given field to get a real bird's-eye view of the work, the culture, and the environment to help you make decisions for yourself and your next steps. These conversations spark new ideas just about every time. Every contact you make can lead to other people who may be looking for someone with your interests, talents, and experience. Plus, most people enjoy telling the story of their professional journey and appreciate the opportunity to relate why they love what they do, something they seldom get asked.

There are really just four simple steps to informational interviewing. Let's say you want to find out about a particular field to figure out potential career moves.

1. List the people you would like to talk to and why—folks you know at least a little or connections you can use to network with friends, colleagues, and acquaintances.

2. Reach out to the ones you are most comfortable with, asking for a ten-minute informational conversation about their careers over coffee or tea. I have almost never been turned down. (If the person doesn't respond, give them another chance by emailing them again. If they don't respond a second time, assume their lives are just crazy busy, and as much as they would like to, they just can't help you at this time. Don't take it personally.)

3. Before the meeting, go back to the person's online info and craft a couple of great questions. Most of the time, you need just one to get things rolling: for example, "I'd love to hear a bit about how you got to where you are today" or "What surprised you about it?" or "What advice would you give someone seeking to enter this realm?"

4. Before the meeting ends, ask if they know of one or two other people you could connect with. Most of the time, names will come up in the course of the conversation, but if not, ask at the end. Be sure to find out if you can reach out directly to those people or need to be introduced by email or phone by your interviewee first. And, of course, don't forget the thank-you note!

Given the statistics, informational interviewing is a phenomenal way to learn about options with respect to your professional journey and to connect with people who may be instrumental in helping you get there.

Whether you are forty, fifty, sixty, or seventy when you send a child off to college, this can be a pivotal moment for you professionally. Every parent I've known ended up engaging more deeply in their world of work. Some did it by investing more energy in colleagues, professional organizations, and the work itself; others changed jobs; some went back to school; yet others retired and started something in a whole new, meaningful field. If you start thinking about this now and planning for the fall, you will be ready to roll soon after college drop-off.

Food for Thought

- Just as your child is contemplating an unknown future, you can take a moment to consider yours.
- Exploring, imagining, and dreaming are not the sole realm of the young.
- As you consider your career and finances, plan to make desired changes in the fall with the tools at your disposal, including informational interviewing, your online presence, and financial advisors.

A Typical College Week: Structurelessness and Serendipity

High school is nothing if not highly structured. Your kids have probably gone from early morning to late evening careening from one activity to the next, barely finding time to eat. With 168 hours in a week, most of their waking hours have been accounted for. Even sleep has taken a back seat to the obligations and hustle and bustle that demanded their attention.

In contrast, as they look at the class schedule they are constructing for the fall, the week may seem eerily empty. Class time takes up only about fifteen hours, a few more for sciences and engineering students—out of 168. What are they going to do with the other 153 hours? This stark reality can be very unsettling, not only to parents, but to the college freshmen themselves. Of course, parents are afraid of different things than their kids are! New first-years are terrified of loneliness, while their parents are wondering what their kids will get up to if they have too much free time on their hands. Or what the heck they're spending all that money on if their child is loafing around a lot.

Indeed, your child is about to transition from a schedule that was compactly arranged in a collaborative way with teachers, guidance counselors, friends, and you to a minimally structured life to which they alone will give form and shape in the coming weeks and months. This transition poses challenges for everyone. It is much more than time management. It is about making sure new college students understand the demands of the landscape they are about to navigate, define their priorities, reassess them often, and grasp the significance of the utter lack of predetermined structure.

Cameron, for instance, had been a child actor since the age of five. His life had been a study in time management, with auditions, plays, movies, commercials, schoolwork, and cello lessons all scrunched into every week, not to mention hours with tutors when he was on the road. When he arrived at college, his first-semester course schedule startled him. Four classes were going to take up only about three hours a day, Monday through Thursday. He hadn't anticipated so much freedom and was thrilled. He immediately auditioned for a number of plays, an a cappella group, and a dance troupe. He got into almost all of them. But by midterms, he was in trouble academically. He knew it, but he didn't want to let anyone know that he was drowning. His academics continued to suffer because he refused to disappoint his new friends in any of the extracurriculars. On the first day of finals, having been up for several days cramming for exams, he walked into his advisor's office, curled up on her couch, and started to sob.

You may think this is an unusual scenario, but it's not. Every semester I work with students who find themselves in this very same situation. Why is this so common? Because class schedules are deceiving. They don't tell you nearly what you need to know. Each class schedule merely reveals the number of hours dedicated to sitting in a lecture hall, classroom, or lab. What is not included in the calculation is the number of hours students are expected to spend—on average—on each course outside of those spaces. Think of the time in class as an initial, skeletal guide that will be filled out with the other meaningful activities that demand their time as much, if not more, as they settle into courses.

For some reason, colleges are quite coy about the hours of out-of-classroom work required to do well in each course. The national guideline indicates that students should plan to spend three hours a week on work outside of class for every credit. Therefore, if they are taking 15 credits (the average needed to complete a 120-credit degree in four years), they should plan for 45 more hours a week on reading, memorizing, writing, studying alone or in groups, presentation practice, problem sets, talking with the professor after class and during office hours, and meeting with teaching assistants. That brings the total weekly commitment to sixty hours: $15 + 45 = 60$. That's already more than the typical full-time job in the United States!

Let's say you hope that they sleep seven hours per night, for a total of forty-nine hours. So, 60 + 49 = 109. We are now up to 109 hours of committed time per week.

Perhaps they'll spend three hours a day going to the dining hall, getting meals, talking with people, and walking back to their room. Add another twenty-one hours (though many new college students spend far more time than this lazing around and chatting over meals). We are now at 130.

If they play a sport or dance or participate in theater, that's another twenty or more hours.

Out of a maximum of 168, there are now 18 hours in a week left for socializing, movies/TV, listening to music, showering, dressing, laundry, and exercising. And we haven't even talked about clubs, errands, and texting friends, not to mention work-study and internships. And talking to you, their parents.

In reality, most students spend fewer than three hours per credit per week on work outside of the classroom because there are just not enough hours in a day. One thing is for sure: They will never feel that there is enough time, so they will end up having to prioritize some activities over others.

The All-Important Fall Schedule

Some colleges have students create their fall course lineup in the summer. Others wait until they are on the ground. If your child doesn't have one yet, it's a great time for them to open the course catalog and construct one, keeping in mind any required first-year courses and their potential areas of study. Whether or not your child has actually selected courses already, however, the following is a really good exercise to prepare for the fall semester:

- For each credit of coursework, add three hours of out-of-class time for reading, writing, and arithmetic, as the old adage goes.
- Add sleep and meals.
- Consider the potential extracurricular activities and build in time for them. They may need to consult the college website or connect with peer advisors on social media or email to get an idea of time commitments for various organizations.
- Remind them to sketch in an internship or work-study job of ten hours a week, if applicable.
- Insert time for showering, dressing, getting to classes, exercising, laundry, and errands.
- How does it look? If it seems crowded, the next step is to help them think through their priorities. Which courses and activities will they give precedence over others when it's crunch time?

When students see the relatively empty initial schedule without doing this exercise, they understandably think, like Cameron, that they are going to have loads of free time, so they sign up for lots of extracurriculars. After all, college is the quintessential period for learning new things that they might not be able to do once they are out in the "real world." Students also reason that engaging in lots of activities will help them find friends quickly. It can naturally be frightening to arrive on a campus where they don't know anyone. But it's useful for them to remember that they will connect with new people everywhere they go: in the dorms, in the classroom, at parties, and in the dining halls, libraries, and lounges. Sure, it takes time. Everyone feels scared and lonely sometimes in the first semester. If they give in to their initial impulse and dive headfirst into a gazillion activities, they will eventually find they have no time to do anything well. This approach can leave students feeling even lonelier than they did before. Not to mention exhausted and defeated.

Likewise, they may feel drawn to enroll in more courses than any advisor, RA, or peer advisor would recommend. After all, college course schedules look like a cakewalk compared to the demands of the high school week. Of course, you and they think they can handle it. Maybe they can, but it is still a bad idea to overload their schedule when they are adjusting to college. Remind them that they have to be able to devote time and energy to every class so that they can learn as much as possible about the subject. If their high school experience conditioned them to think of education as a kind of race—*because* of the race to get into college—remind them that those days are largely over. They are not in a race anymore! This is a time for them to dig into the material of each topic and to get to know the field and the faculty who have devoted their lives to it. In other words, they have to rethink things to include more room than ever before per course.

Resisting the Urge to Load Up

To help your child resist the urge to sign up for more than they should:

- Suggest that they consider adjusting to college as one course in the first semester—which means that they are already overloaded a bit because they are taking one more than required, which at most colleges is four or five.
- Recommend that they sign up for just one extracurricular activity until they have the lay of the land.

- If they find they have downtime, with nothing scheduled, they should not equate that with failure. The free time will vanish.
- There will be many instances later on in the semester when they will wish they had some breathing room. Then they will think back fondly on these moments of having nothing to do.

Another common misconception among both students and their parents is that students should get the distribution or core requirements out of the way as quickly as possible. Accordingly, they fill up their fall schedule with them, in spite of their advisor's guidance. The problem with this is that the first four semesters at most liberal arts colleges ought to be utilized in a strategic way to nail down the major(s) and minor(s), where they will spend more of their time in the junior and senior years.

In fact, most colleges divide the curriculum into three parts: one for distribution or core requirements, one for the major, and a third for electives, minors, programs, certificates, et cetera. I call this "the rule of thirds." The first third are courses that the college deems necessary to produce well-rounded, well-educated citizens. The second third enables students to do an in-depth study of at least one field where they will hopefully find a supportive academic home. And the third is up to them. So it may be helpful to think of distributing the courses into three buckets over four years. There is plenty of time to do it all, and balance is the key.

If your child ends up taking too many courses right away that are designed to meet requirements, which is admittedly very tempting, they may struggle to choose a major by the end of sophomore year. This is one of the biggest academic mistakes freshmen make. If, on the other hand, they skip them and choose courses that will help them select a major, the junior and senior years will be overly heavy with required courses, which will prevent them from being able to spend as much energy as they should on coursework in the major, on the thesis and other capstone experiences, and on collecting other credentials they want to accrue before graduating. Again, prioritization and balance are essential, as with so many things in life.

Consider Lauren, an ambitious freshman from California. She was really eager to make the most of college, and for her this translated into scheduling every minute of every day. Needless to say, partway through the first semester she was dog-tired. She met with her advisor to plan the coming semester and was surprised when her advisor, noting how overwrought she seemed, suggested she schedule some free time in her weeks for serendipity. "Serendipity? What for?" Lauren replied. The advisor's answer: "Because overscheduling precludes you from being open to chance, to experience the unexpected, the new, and the surprising things in life." She was skeptical but decided to give it a try—at least to see if she would feel less frazzled next semester. Weeks into the spring term, Lauren bounded into her advisor's office to announce that "leaving time for serendipity" had paid off. While sitting outside the library on a bench enjoying the sunshine, she got into a conversation with a graduate student who needed a research assistant in East Asian politics, which was right up her alley. Because she had left room in her schedule, she was able to devote several hours a week to this unexpected opportunity. She and the graduate student ended up publishing the research in a well-respected journal, so Lauren had her first publication before the end of junior year.

Scheduling Strategies

- At first, the fall college schedule will likely appear very empty, with "only" fifteen to twenty hours of class time per week.

- This is a deceiving number, since each course credit should require at least three hours of time a week outside of the classroom. A three-credit course could mean at least nine additional hours of work, if not more, depending on the nature of it.
- It's best for freshmen not to commit to more than one extra-curricular activity in the first semester.
- Getting used to college should be counted as one additional course.
- Everyone experiences loneliness and down moments in the first semester. Your child is not alone. There are lots of sources of support and comfort on every college campus. Helping them reach out is key.
- Leaving time in a student's schedule for serendipity can have unexpectedly wonderful results.

It's Your Summer for Change, Too

Whether it's your first or last child who's about to start college, their departure will at minimum create a change in your family life. There are two important initial facts to keep in mind as you think about restructuring your days. The first is that habit-changing and habit-building take time—a lot of it. Some researchers have shown that a few habits can be changed in as little as three weeks, but others take months, if not years. What is the habit you are about to change now? You, as a dutiful, devoted parent, have a well-established pattern of thinking of your child's needs first and foremost. Perhaps even to the exclusion of your own at many moments in the past eighteen or more years. This is completely normal and warranted, not to mention commendable. How could you have done otherwise? Your child's happiness and well-being have been paramount. But now, knowing that you have done all you can, the best thing you can do for yourself and your child is to make yourself a priority. It's time to begin to change your habits of mind and action.

I'm not suggesting you abandon your child. Far from it! But knowing that your child will be off to college soon, you will benefit immeasurably by starting to find new ways of thinking and acting, just as the new college freshman will. Being intentional and starting slowly will help. It's not to say that you will immediately crave a day of doing nothing, but that's not a bad goal, either.

Obviously I am encouraging you to think of this change as positive, not as a gaping hole in the fabric of your life! Facing a loss offers us the perfect moment to start establishing new patterns. When you have a free second in your day when you naturally find yourself picking up the phone to call or text your kid, don't. Instead, contact a friend, make an appointment you have put off, or just look up at the sky and daydream. Directing your energy to people and things other than your daughter or son will be hard, but if you start now, you will have come a long way by the time you get to drop-off day and that tearful farewell. Not only will this open up new paths and exciting activities, but it also will fill the emptiness you may experience once the semester is under way and that kid is no longer there to feed, move from place to place, and talk to every day.

Whenever I tell the story of Eric, people think I'm making it up. But I'm not, and it's not all that unusual. He was a lawyer who had just retired to move to his son Ralph's college town. He got his hands on the syllabi, bought the books for all of his son's fall courses, and sat at the back of the lecture halls if he could do so unnoticed. (This college invited community members to audit lectures, so Eric wasn't the only non-college-age person there.) A few weeks into the term, he had a moment of realization when Ralph's advisor let him know that editing his son's papers was putting Ralph in danger of academic suspension for a year. Eric began to ask himself what the heck he was doing. His marriage was falling apart, his son had less and less time to spend with him, and even the always accommodating advisor had started looking at him in disbelief. With a heavy heart, Eric gave up the apartment, moved back home, and began to devote his energy to his spouse and a new nonprofit.

I'm not unique in seeing this kind of thing happen. Every college administrator can share numerous stories of the parent who gives up his own life and adopts the eighteen-year-old's new one. Maybe you're not headed down this road, but to be sure you transition to this new normal, try to catch yourself as you wonder what your kid is up to or as you do yet one more thing for your child, and redirect your focus at least a couple of times a day. In this way, you head down the path of breaking old habits and creating new ones. It's the perfect time to embrace new habits of mind. By catching yourself, rerouting your attention to something other than your child, and taking steps toward others in your near and distant communities, you will begin to open yourself up to new possibilities. It's absolutely the right time to think about your habits of mind and action as just that—habits that can be broken. They have served you well for so long, but soon they will cease to do so. Any action you take now to reroute your energies will benefit you in the long run. You will feel less of a loss and you will have begun to connect in intentional and generative ways with new acquaintances and old friends, thereby fortifying your social life and engagement.

In addition to the process of habit-breaking and habit establishment, the second important fact to keep in mind is that brains, and therefore our lives, are elastic. Enriching your environment enhances your ability to learn and live enthusiastically and well. If you approach creative pathfinding with that perspective, you will find it is easier to break out of old patterns that may have become unproductive ruts. Since you might not be used to thinking about new and different undertakings as possibilities for you, it could take a while before you will be able to imagine them for yourself. Be patient. They will come. You are beginning a new phase of your life where you are making time for and putting energy into yourself.

Time and time again, researchers identify five factors, in particular, that make a decisive difference in our efforts to learn new things and explore untaken paths. If you pay attention to these on a regular basis, you will set yourself up for a happier, more fulfilled transition.

1. *Challenge yourself.* Encounter something new every day, whether it's a crossword puzzle, an article in a magazine, or a tough recipe. Stretch your psychological and adventure muscles, at least briefly on a regular basis.
2. *Encounter newness.* We all fall into ruts, preferring to spend time with familiar people, follow routines, and go to our favorite places time and again. Make opportunities to break out of those. Speak to someone new at work, try an unfamiliar activity, or go somewhere in your town where you haven't been.
3. *Nutrition.* When you feed yourself, you feed your brain. It's tempting to give in to the convenience and comfort of takeout or prepared foods when you are pressed for time. The higher the quality of the food you eat, the better off your brain will be and the more joyfully you will live life.
4. *Movement.* You will not be surprised to hear that exercise finds itself among these five factors. But it means more than running to the car in the morning or rushing home from work!
5. *Love and other positive emotions.* Many experiments show that positive emotions have a strengthening effect not only on our brains but also on our immune and other bodily systems. If you have old friends you haven't contacted in a while, take ten minutes and give them a call. Reach out to family members you adore but haven't seen regularly so that you can feel loved and remember how much you love them. Outreach, especially at this juncture, can generate positive energy!

For a number of parents a decisive moment comes when they consider paths not taken earlier in life. I know one dad, Tom, who had a knot in his stomach as his last child prepared for college. He was afraid to admit it, but he suspected he was going to fall apart when she left. But when he drove away from the drop-off, he felt an unanticipated sense of exhilaration. He couldn't account for it at first and thought he was in denial, but then it slowly dawned on him that he would have the chance to engage in politics again. He hadn't been able to do anything at all while he was raising the kids except sign a few petitions. But now he leapt into community political races to help and joined organizations that worked to advance his favorite local causes.

Another parent, a mom named Dorothea, actually sat down and made a list of things she wanted to try and habits she'd long ago gotten out of. When she looked at these "paths not taken" notes, she spotted the theme of writing. She had always composed poems, silly ones, and had spent a lot of time journaling, but she'd never taken time to indulge in these happy pastimes. She went online and discovered that her town's library offered several writing classes, and she has since signed up, cautiously optimistic that this might be a productive new direction for her.

If you are like many parents, your community engagement and social life have been intertwined with that of your children. School parents you've known over the years, carpoolers you depended on, families you met at sports events and performances, parents of play-date buddies and religious youth group companions—you have been surrounded by them, have called and texted them, and may follow them on social media sites. But soon you won't have to be in touch with them anymore. The reason for your communications will cease to exist. You will have choices to make. Sure, you will stay in touch with one or two of them. But now it's the moment to forge new paths of your own choosing. How liberating!

Breaking old habits, establishing new ones, and cultivating a personally enriched landscape will help you build the equivalent of new synapses of activity in your brain. The change begins now, gradually, step by step, and will yield positive and productive results.

Summertime Reflection

- Spend some time thinking about your social life. How much of it involves your child, your child's friends and their families?
- Once your child goes to college, do you think you would like your social life to change?
- Give equal time to thinking about your community engagement. Does much of it stem from child-rearing activities? Are there aspects of it you would like to alter in the fall?
- Are there friends and relatives you have missed and would like to reconnect with?
- Are there community organizations that interest you?
- Are there options in your local area that you haven't had time to read about and consider?

You're understandably anxious about getting this new phase started, and the summertime anticipation can be difficult. So use this time to dream intentionally about these important and exciting possibilities.

CHAPTER 5

The Dog Days

Gulp—it's August, the last month you will all be living under the same roof, at least for a while. In and around a summer job, your rising freshman may be busy packing, or thinking about packing, and shopping for what to pack and perhaps already communicating with their roommate (and discussing what to pack and shop for). But they'll also be in the throes of protracted goodbyes with their high school friends and saying farewell—in ways both small and large—to their high school selves.

As adults know well, goodbyes can be tricky. For rising college freshmen, they are emotionally and physically draining because they not only anticipate cataclysmic change in their lives but trigger a gnawing anticipation of loss. Parents, siblings, schoolmates, neighbors, sports teams, music teachers, religious guides, employers, and even local shopkeepers will no longer be around. And they don't yet know the people who will surround them daily. The time between leaving and establishing a new home and social circle on a college campus can seem like an infinity. Saying goodbye to you comes soon enough, but for now helping your child be intentional about their goodbyes ensures they do it well. They need to understand who they want and need to stay in touch with once they move away. These will be the people they contact first when they come back for breaks, Thanksgiving, and, possibly, next summer. So work with your child, if they will allow it, to bring a measure of intentionality to the good-bye coffees, lunches, dinners, and parties.

Helping Your Child Prepare to Say Goodbye

This list of questions will help you guide your child through purposeful farewells.

- Who are the most important friends?
- Which relatives must get and deserve some attention at this time?
- Are there family friends who should be included in a farewell event?
- To whom does your child owe thanks? Expressing gratitude for any assistance they received from people in their circles can be powerful and make them feel good about this whole process.
- Would a single farewell gathering at the end of the summer be best so that they can get it all done in one fell swoop?
- What sorts of time and money are on hand for this sort of thing? Does any of it require travel? How much notice do you need to give people?

With the prospect of loss in their future, goodbyes are a meaningful way to ensure that relationships are maintained in anticipation of the inevitable distance. The people your child makes time to see will be grateful and understand their importance in your child's life when extra time and effort are put into saying goodbye and expressing gratitude before the move.

Make a Communication Plan!

When Ben and Jo got home from the airport after traveling to college drop-off with their daughter, Matilda, they turned on their cell-phones expecting a barrage of texts from her updating them on how everything was going. After all, it had been eight hours since they left campus. But there was nothing. At first they thought the problem was that they were still on the tarmac, but everyone else on the plane was already busy texting people. What was going on? They panicked. As they hurried toward the baggage claim to get their luggage (most of which was filled with stuff that didn't fit into Matilda's dorm room), they began calling her obsessively, to no avail. They scoured their carry-on bags for information about campus emergency contacts and found the number of the crisis team manager, who answered immediately. When he heard the parents' concern, he immediately recognized the phenomenon: parents without a communication plan with their new college students. He promised he would find Matilda immediately and have her get in touch with them. When he found her, she was enjoying a late-night jamboree on the lawn with all of the other freshmen.

Some version of this story takes place on every college campus at least several times after parent drop-off. Given the closeness of so many parents and their children these days, it's surprising it doesn't happen more often. Matilda—appropriately—had merely been swept up in the orientation programs, setting up her room, meeting new people, and discovering her new campus. She was so excited to finally be at college that she hadn't even realized how much time had passed since she had checked in with her parents.

Another version of this story plays itself out when, believe it or not, parents ask someone on campus to make sure their child gets out of bed in time for their first class of the day. Some mean the first day or week. Others mean the whole semester. The parents say they don't want to do it themselves because they think their child will see them as intrusive or mistrustful of them. Even now when almost everyone has a cellphone alarm clock, parents still ask. In these cases, what parents really want is an adult to make contact with their child on a regular basis in their stead to make sure they are okay. They are worried about not being able to see them every day to gauge how they are doing, especially in a transition as infamously tough as this one. That's understandable, but this is a transition that your child can and should do on their own.

For many parents, one of the hardest things is just this: not knowing where your kid is for long stretches of time and not being able to see in person how they are doing every day. This can be pretty anxiety-provoking and even frightening. Families that come up with a communication plan ahead of time and adjust it as needed over the initial months are able to reduce the nervousness and fear a great deal.

The first step is to settle on how and when you will talk and/or text after you leave campus. Keep in mind that the orientation schedules are demanding, and it may not always be possible for new students to access their phones, especially if they are involved in a long scavenger hunt, watching a theater piece on sexual assault prevention, participating in a faculty-led conversation on values, or enjoying a comedic piece of musical theater put on by orientation leaders. All of these things and more await new college students, and the schedules are designed to keep them busy from morning to night—with the idea that this is the one and only time the college will have their undivided attention, so they have to give them all of the information they could possibly need to succeed and ensure they feel welcomed. Plus, colleges are seriously focused on avoiding overly exuberant behavior when these hundreds of seventeen- and eighteen-year-olds come together for the first time for days without any academic obligations. The drinking and drugging that go on during orientation are notoriously difficult to tame. If students are kept occupied all waking hours, college administrators reason, the opportunity for mischief is reduced. When a campus gets through orientation with no alcohol- or other drug-related ambulance calls, it considers itself lucky.

Also keep in mind that the best-laid plans sometimes go awry! By all means, make a plan for the first contact, but then be prepared to be flexible. And patient.

The next step in the communication plan is to consider the frequency and means of being in touch once classes begin. Settle on a plan, but know it will probably change as your child's obligations shift in the first term.

It is not unusual for families to agree to share their electronic calendars with one another, which is becoming easier all the time, especially now that many campuses have switched over to Google Calendar. If you fall into this category, it is advisable to think about why you would want to continue to do so. It may be that it makes it easier to stay in touch, but it's also possible that there are less healthy motivations attached to it. Being honest with yourself and your teenager will go a long way toward deepening the relationship during the impending separation.

Finally, talk together through the steps you would take if you were gravely concerned about your child's well-being. Your child needs to know that you might sound the proverbial alarm if too much time passes without contact. And it'll be immensely helpful to all to be forthright about what constitutes "too much time."

Of course, sometimes these plans do more than placate nervous parents; they save lives. Bernard had faced some depression in his teens, but the family had great hopes for him in a new environment, away from some of the things that had caused him misery in high school. They desperately wanted to give him space once he was at college, but also worried about how he was adjusting and whether he was taking his medications. They had agreed to be in touch by text every other day and by phone once a week. They had alerted the school to Bernard's medical needs and, through that process, had met his advisor, who, as it turned out, was a staff professional (rather than a faculty advisor) who had been trained in crisis management and even served on the behavioral intervention team. Together, they made a contingency plan—the parents would call Bernard's advisor if they didn't hear from him for over a week. That moment came in his sophomore year, when the depression became so debilitating that Bernard stopped leaving his room. The system they put in place in his first year ended up saving his second year.

Once you have a plan in place for the first contact and the first weeks of school as well as the emergency contact plan, you are golden.

You may think you have all this beat since you use one of those handy apps that show you your child's (or at least their phone's) location whenever you want. If so, do you think it would be healthy at this point to rethink your reliance on this? Obviously, I think so, but this is probably a good topic for you and your child to discuss in the lead-up to move-in.

The All-Important Health Network

One of the things everyone dreads when moving to a new place is assembling new health professionals. Even if you only need a general practitioner, the search can be daunting and laborious. When students move to college, it's always beneficial and sometimes downright essential for them and their parents to know what medical services are available and to get a health network in place before move-in. What services has the student needed on a regular basis in the past few years? Are there medications that need to be resupplied periodically? Where do students get their prescriptions filled? What medical personnel does the college employ? Where do students go when their needs can't be met on campus? Which local hospitals work closely with the university? Now's the time to sort these things out.

If you are worried about your child's ability to maintain a medically prescribed routine, it is essential for them to set up an appointment to meet a healthcare professional during orientation and explain the history and ongoing needs. You can go, too, if your child is okay with that. Once the health services office has everything on file, it will be better equipped to handle any future emergencies. Even if there are no current medical issues, do both of you a favor and learn about the facilities and the best way to make appointments. College students are notorious for exchanging germs. They live in close quarters and aren't always the most hygienic. We have all heard stories of flu, pinkeye, and mononucleosis outbreaks among close buddies in dorms. If your child wakes up with crusty red eyes, she will want to know how to get care as quickly as possible.

It is always advisable to be honest with the college ahead of time about a student's physical and psychological needs. I cannot stress this enough. Families sometimes believe they should do their utmost to hide conditions from school officials. Maybe they fear that the offer of admission will be revoked or that their child will be marked in some way. (I can assure you that it would be unethical and illegal to do either of those, and just about every institution of higher learning has high ethical standards and legal teams that do not need any additional work.) Hiding medical needs is precisely the opposite of what a college hopes. Believe me, they have heard and seen everything. Your child's issues are probably not unique or even unusual. Once they know what a student needs, they can support them better throughout their college years.

Consider Leslie, a freshman who had been treated for schizophrenia for several years. She had not revealed her diagnosis or treatment prior to arrival. Nor had she tried to find out what medical facilities were at her disposal. She viewed college as a new chapter and desperately wanted to leave the old trappings of her life behind, including most of her medications. She soon began to feel weird but didn't know where to turn. She was going through withdrawal and experiencing the reemergence of her condition all at once. Shortly after classes began, her RA thought she was acting a little strangely, so he tried to talk with her. He was concerned enough that he mentioned it to the class dean when he met with her about his semester. She had no prior medical information either, so they speculated together that Leslie was probably just under stress of the transition. Had Leslie prepared herself and her institution, the dean would immediately have suspected that something more serious was up, and gotten Leslie help. As it was, she suffered from her medication withdrawal and illness until her behavior became outrageous: She was throwing lamps out of a tenth-story window. Not only was she upsetting people, but she was now dangerous. When Public Safety spotted the lamps falling from the upper floor of a dormitory, Leslie finally got the right help. Unfortunately, the situation now involved the fire and police departments, an ambulance, a hospital, and, eventually, the student conduct office.

Why this focus on health networks? Moving to a new place, making new friends, learning the terrain, making academic, social, and other sorts of decisions—none of this is easy. In fact, this might be hands-down the most stressful situation any young person has encountered so far in their short life. Even if they are thrilled to go to college, change entails stress, which can exacerbate the smallest of medical problems and even cause new ones. If every new college student knew where to turn and did so when they had an inkling they needed physical or psychological help, everyone would benefit.

Colleges and universities are now laser-focused on these issues. They have started to talk about "wellness" rather than health on the idea that while health is merely the absence of illness, wellness is the cultivation of a health-maintaining lifestyle. But why are they so fixated on health and well-being? There are a number of reasons. One goes back a couple of decades. In the spring of 2000, a nineteen-year-old sophomore at MIT named Elizabeth Shin set herself on fire. She had seen multiple mental health specialists and threatened suicide a number of times, but the school had not notified the family because Elizabeth was over eighteen. Her parents filed a wrongful-death suit, charging that MIT was responsible. The case settled out of court about six years later, but the ripple effects of the suit were felt across the nation. That one case many years ago led colleges to begin reconsidering the answers to myriad questions and also thrust into relief the ever-increasing mental illness issues on our nation's college campuses.

As a result of the Shin case (and others, including the April 2007 Virginia Tech shootings), many institutions dramatically changed their policies and procedures with respect to student healthcare communications. Parents are brought onboard much earlier than they used to be. Some information about students is also carefully shared with more officials on campus to create a network of people knowledgeable about a student's needs in case of emergency. And students are asked to be more forthcoming so that the people in charge of their welfare can take good care of them.

You might ask why a college would hesitate to contact you if your child was suffering in some way. It's a reasonable question. After all, you have been loving and caring for this child since birth. That doesn't end just because they have started this new chapter in their lives. But colleges are beholden to federal laws that protect your child's educational and medical records from disclosure once they reach the magic age of eighteen. So, what exactly are the responsibilities of the institution if your child is ill, gets hurt, or tries to hurt themselves or others? These are gruesome topics, but colleges contend with them every day, unfortunately.

The most important factor in the way that schools think about medical information is HIPAA. With respect to the rest, the major determinant is the Family Educational Rights and Privacy Act (FERPA, also known as the Buckley Amendment), passed in 1974 and subsequently modified several times. FERPA transfers the right to access records from the parent to the student when the student goes to college. While your child's elementary, middle, and high schools have probably taken great pains to engage you in their successes and challenges so far, a law now prevents the next school from doing the same. It's complicated, but the bottom line is that college officials can share information about your child with one another as long as they have a "legitimate educational interest," which, as you can imagine, is subject to broad interpretation. But they are not allowed to share it with you unless your child gives explicit permission or in the case of "health and safety emergencies." Again, these are terms that are subjective and differentially interpreted.

The FERPA Muddle

Every college grapples with FERPA compliance as much as parents struggle to understand it. A common question: Why wouldn't a college share grades with you if you are footing the bill? You have been caring for this human for eighteen years, so how is it within a college's rights to cut you off from academic progress data and information? Whether we like it or not, it is the law. But take heart! Every college has a FERPA release form, which your child can sign to give the college permission to share any information your new college student lists on that sheet of paper (or electronic PDF). The permission is usually time-bound, so be sure to check the expiration date. It could be a month, a semester, a year, or more, depending on the form and your child's preference.

In the wake of the Shin case and others, university administrators, provosts, and presidents are wrestling constantly with the boundaries between the confidentiality of a legally protected college student and the wisdom of engaging their families. Most now have protocols in place to notify a parent in the case of danger to self or others, meaning a student is hurting themselves or there is some reason to believe that they are going to inflict harm on someone else. So they may not call you if your kid gets strep throat or breaks a bone, but will if life is at stake. Other colleges put protocols in place so that you are notified for every hospital incident or hospitalization, with student permission.

If this is of particular concern to you, by all means ask the health services office for their policy on contacting parents in the event of student illness. (Some colleges won't contact you even if your child is not yet eighteen.) Remember that college health services staff are beholden to the HIPAA privacy rule just as any other medical facility is, so it will be up to your child to give the college permission to contact you and share medical information with you. If there is a serious health issue from the outset, see if there are forms your new college student can fill out to give health services staff permission to reach out to you and provide you medical status and updates as needed.

So, let's say you are ready to reach out to the college to share previously safeguarded information about your child's health. Contacting someone on campus in August may not be as easy as you would like. July and early August are the only times of the year when campus employees can take real vacations. If move-in begins in late August or early September, mid-August will find staff flocking back to their desks, so your emails will be answered more quickly then than in the six weeks prior to that. If those offices will be open during orientation, see what you need to do to schedule an appointment during that time, or see what workshops are offered, and plan it for a time when your child is free.

Getting Your Head Around Healthcare

Some useful questions to consider with your child:

- What conditions are they presently being treated for? How long will any present medication supply last? When will they need to see a doctor for a prescription renewal?
- Are there issues that your child might have that have not yet been addressed?
- What campus medical facilities are available to undergraduates? Where are they? What do they cost?
- Which physical or mental health services are outsourced? To where?
- Did you opt for the college medical insurance? What is the name of the insurance company, what is the policy number, and what does it cover? Are the doctors from home covered? Are any outsourced services to the local area covered?
- Did you waive the student insurance? If so, can your child see healthcare practitioners in the local area? What choices will they have?
- What medical information could help the college support your child well?
- Is there anything in the realm of physical or mental health that might prevent your child from devoting himself 100 percent to the more than full-time job of being a college student? If there is, you ought to connect with a campus healthcare practitioner to discuss your concerns and the possible ways to manage it.

The Keys to Packing

Whenever you find good articles about packing for a trip, they include one important command: Lay out what you think you need, and then edit, edit, edit. I have found this true of college move-in prep as well. Dorm rooms are small, and they get ever-more crowded over the course of the nine months students inhabit them. Books, papers, computers, sometimes TVs still, clothes, rugs, refrigerators, hotplates, coffeepots, cereal boxes, bottles of Gatorade and other beverages, dishes, and swag, swag, swag—water bottles, tote bags, lanyards, and other stuff bearing the name and emblem of the school. So the residences are never as tidy as they are when you finish setting them up before rushing off to the next orientation event, at least not until the students move out, when they create mountains of stuff outside the dorms destined for recycling at local homeless shelters or the trash. Some families go to great lengths—with bedding, rugs, curtains—but more often than not, even these magazine-worthy efforts end up messy and cluttered shortly thereafter. I would stick to the motto "Less is more."

Taking Some Home Along to College

Many incoming students bring photos of family, friends, pets, and home to mount on a bulletin board. Some families make a collage together to hang on the wall. It provides a warm reminder that the freshman is loved when they inevitably face some lonely moments in the first few months as they make new friends and establish new social circles.

Not that tidiness is everything. But in my time on campuses, I have seen and heard some horrific things, from salmonella detected on unwashed spoons to surfaces holding all kinds of bodily fluids for longer than you care to imagine. Students are busy. One thing that can help them maintain order is the simplicity that comes with minimalism. They need far less stuff than they think.

You may be tempted to do the packing yourself, but there is a lot to be said for the child taking the time and thought to do this on their own. Not only is it a measurable step toward independence, but they will use this as an opportunity to think about what is important to them to take and to leave behind, and how they want to present themselves in their new home. If they haven't lived away from home yet and haven't had the opportunity to pack for trips much, this will be a steep learning curve. But give them the chance to work it through, and then offer help later on before the packing of the suitcases and/or the vehicle begins.

The students who travel to campus by plane or bus are among the luckier ones because they are forced to make tougher decisions before boarding. The families who arrive by SUV and van rarely leave campus with empty vehicles. The stuff just won't fit into the room, especially given that so many colleges are doubling, tripling, and quadrupling up the beds in every room to save money.

Travel experts love the three-times-three rule: Three bottoms and three tops make nine outfits. For college, I like the seven-times-seven rule: Seven bottoms and seven tops make forty-nine outfits. Most students spend their days in jeans or sweats and T-shirts anyway (many of which they will acquire in the first few weeks of school), because comfort is essential for all that rushing around. One nice outfit for the first semester will suffice. They don't have many opportunities for dressing up before they come home at Thanksgiving, and by then they will have the lay of the land and know what they want to schlep back to campus and/or what they need for the months ahead.

Now is the time for your child to start laying out everything they think they need and want at college. Anywhere will do. This is exhausting work, so have them do it once, and then leave it overnight.

The next day, have them tackle it again. And edit, edit, edit. The process will take at least a week, and be forewarned that there may be tears (yours, theirs, or both), since packing is both frustrating *and* a visible marker of their departure.

Packing Tips

- Given that toiletries and food are available in every college town, I recommend not packing those. I wouldn't waste precious space on them. When you get to campus, ask where the nearest drug store or dollar store is and stock up then.
- There is time to order notebooks, pens, pencils, et cetera, when they get to campus. College bookstores are notoriously overpriced, so you may want to order from a cheaper online site.
- Seven bottoms and seven tops should suffice, in addition to seven days' worth of undergarments.
- One or two sweaters, a sweatshirt, a vest, and a winter coat (depending on the climate) should be enough.
- Sneakers, shower shoes, flip-flops, winter and rain boots (if needed), and a nice pair of shoes should do.
- One nice outfit might be needed for the random dinner or event.
- Bedding: Most colleges strike deals with big-box stores to allow students to order online and pick up what they need when they get there. Some even deliver the items to the dorm. The last thing you'll probably want to do at drop-off is to schlep off to Bed Bath & Beyond to buy bedding. So, if you are like me, just order it online unless you are sending them with bedding from home. Look up the size of the bed,

though! Most colleges use a 96-inch mattress. You won't need more than one or two sets of sheets, pillowcases, and pillows. Curtains are not necessary, but are a nice added touch if you are so inclined.

- When it comes to electronics, be sure to check out the college's guidelines. Insurance policies and other practicalities restrict campus electronics. If your child uses the wrong kind of toaster or microwave, high fines could be in their future. Televisions are becoming scarcer and scarcer, since most students watch shows on their computers, tablets, or phones. Your child ought to check with the roommates to see if anyone plans to bring one.

- Computers can be a tough call. Do you spring for a new one or let them take the old one? Do they need one at all? Almost every student arrives on campus these days with their own, but it doesn't have to be new; it just has to function. Unless there are specific needs (like programs for engineering or architecture), any computer ought to do. Don't take a printer until you find out if the campus provides printing credits. Most give students a number of pages per semester for no extra charge, and that will probably suffice.

- Beyond clothes and electronics, not much should be needed. They will soon acquire books, swag, and toiletries—so much that the room will be unrecognizable if you come back for Parents' Weekend in the fall.

- You may want to take note of the instructions regarding the receipt of packages on campus. Some students ship quite a lot to themselves, but not all campuses have the room to hold hundreds of packages all summer long, so they may not be willing to receive packages until a certain date. Also be sure to pay attention to the mailing address and the distance from the package pickup to the dorm.

Seriously, Don't Ignore the Residential Policies Manual

Every college has a handbook of rules and regulations, but almost no one reads them before arriving, much less before making the deposit. Why would you? It sounds more boring than the owner's manual for your iron. But much of what you find there will help you plan ahead.

- What electric items are permitted?
- Can students have a refrigerator? Are there restrictions on size or type?
- What is the alcohol policy? What are the penalties for violating it?
- Is smoking permitted in the dorms? Near the dorms?
- Are students allowed to cook? Are hotplates okay?
- Are candles allowed?
- Is there a guest policy?
- What furniture does the college provide? Can a student bring his or her own bed? How about a loft? What size sheets are needed?
- Can they play sports in the halls? (Probably not, and I've known plenty of students who received a warning from the student conduct office for this one.)
- Where is the laundry room? What does it cost? Is detergent available in the laundry room?
- Where do they buy groceries and sundries?
- What do they do if the heat stops working?
- Is there air-conditioning?
- How big is the room? Can they paint it? Put nails in the walls? What if they do?
- How about pets? Emotional support animals?
- Where are bikes kept? How do they register them?

- Are cars allowed for freshmen? Is parking available? Other class years?
- Are grills available?
- Is there roof access?
- What about summer storage? Summer housing?
- Is housing open during the fall, winter, and spring breaks or does everyone have to leave? If students are able to stay between terms, is there an extra cost involved?
- Does the university cover any losses due to theft, water damage, et cetera? Do you need renter's insurance? Or do you already have a policy that covers this?
- What happens if a student violates rules? Do they stand to lose their on-campus housing?

If every incoming freshman and their parents would read through the handbook just once before arriving on campus, they would duck a lot of heartache and conflict. I cannot tell you how many students arrive on campuses with an SUV full of items that have to be driven home again because they are not permitted or do not fit. Even more frequently, students get into some sort of disciplinary issues because they violate rules out of ignorance. Avoiding this is simple. Just have them read the rules booklet online. It may take forty-five minutes to an hour, but the payoff is big.

The Final Must: Rest, Rest, and More Rest

While your soon-to-be-college freshman is planning farewells and packing, there is one more thing he must be doing: sleeping. Students typically arrive at college in a state of utter physical and psychological depletion. If they don't recharge over the summer, they are particularly at risk in the short term for perceiving excessive emotional drama where there is already enough realistic emotional drama to go around. In the long term, the outcome is far worse. They've been working hard and moving fast and are *physically* tired from the accumulated exertion of the past few years. They have had to keep up community service, athletics and other activities, schoolwork, a job, and extracurriculars. They have tended to family relationships, had some friendship drama, and visited campuses for pre-frosh weekends. And they are *psychologically* fatigued from wrapping up a long chapter of their lives and preparing to open a new one. Of course they are exhausted.

So, what do they do now? They have been on automatic for so long that slowing down, much less stopping completely, hasn't seemed possible. *But if they haven't done so already, now is the time. They must stop moving, sit down, rest, nap, and sleep.* Just as I emphasized in Chapter 3 when they were finishing up high school, the very first thing any college-bound student should do right before college move-in is sleep a lot.

If possible, let your child sleep until they wake up naturally. Make sure everyone in the household knows that they shouldn't be awakened, that they will appear when they wake up on their own without alarm clocks. Have them turn off their computer and phone—or, better yet, put their electronics in a different room. And see if everyone would be okay with keeping the noise level down so that your child can sleep relatively undisturbed. Just let them sleep.

Of course, eating healthfully will help as well. During this period, see if there is any way to avoid extra-stressful situations. Encourage them to be kind to themselves. If they have a job, perhaps the boss can adjust the schedule to accommodate the need for rest.

The risks of sleep deprivation and perpetual exhaustion are many, and they include irritability, anger, depression, weight gain, other health issues, increased incidence of injuries and accidents, overuse of stimulants (caffeine, alcohol, and other drugs), and more. The short- and long-term risks of sleep deprivation are not worth the potential immediate gains!

A Few Quick Reminders

- This is the time to plan farewells in such a way that they help your child prioritize the people to stay in touch with once they move.
- Planning how and how often you are going to communicate after drop-off and beyond prevents misunderstandings and, in some cases, panic.
- Make sure you and your child have set up the health network on campus.
- Packing well requires time and editing, editing, editing. They don't need much, and the less they have, the better off they will be.
- This is also the month for sleeping so that your child arrives on campus refreshed and physically and psychologically ready to make the transition and good decisions.

Saying Goodbye, Saying Hello

Goodbyes are so hard. And this one is particularly momentous. Your child is launching. You may be ready to crawl into a hole at the thought. Or you may be secretly thrilled. Or both. Either way, the moment of final farewell is one that chokes up even the most stoic of humans. But it's done in an instant. We might work ourselves up thinking that this moment is a big deal, and it is in our minds, but it is so fleeting! Plus, as you are saying goodbye to your child and a long era of child-rearing, you are also saying hello to your life after child launch. It may sound trite, but remembering the old adage "When one door closes, another opens" will help. You are about to enter a new chapter, and it can be thrilling. You have done a great job getting your child to this point. Now it's your turn! Say goodbye with a big hug and kiss, and let them go so that they can get on with imagining and building their new life while you do the same with yours.

Bob and Kristi had been married for thirty-five years when they sent the last of their three children off to college. They had dreaded this moment for years, since their lives had been built around raising these three wonderful humans. They had had their share of loss and hardships, but they felt secure in the knowledge that they had provided their children with a well-rounded, solid ethical and educational foundation. So why the angst? Their careers were thriving, their financial strain would soon be alleviated, their children had the love and support of an extended albeit quirky family. And they were healthy. The truth was that they simply feared the change to their mornings, their evenings, and their weekends. What would they do now without children to feed, drive around, and help with homework? What would they talk about? The anxiety got to such a high level that they each entered therapy. The solution, it turned out, was pretty easy for them. After some in-depth conversations at a newly established weekly date night, they realized that they had dreamed of spending time in two ways: on beaches and with a dog. With stretched finances, beach vacations had always been out of the question, but Kristi's brother had just moved to Florida, so they asked him if they could visit. Her brother was overjoyed that someone would make the trek down south from New England, so they planned two long weekends well in advance to reduce the costs. As for the dog, they began a series of informational conversations with friends and co-workers and learned about breeds, animal shelters, and dog training and care. It just so happened that the area near Kristi's brother's house had a rescue shelter for their chosen breed, a puli, so they were able to combine their first beach vacation since their honeymoon with finding a dog in need of a home.

I love this (true) story because it exemplifies that *this is absolutely not rocket science*. It's about mindful intentionality. We are granted an unknown number of minutes on the planet. How we choose to spend them is up to us. When a big change is staring us down, we can take that as an opportunity to review, imagine, revise, and plan. Of course, your heart might ache. But you can fill it with new love and experiences, regardless of your means.

If you're at all like so many of the parents I meet and talk to on campuses, it's likely that you have focused on your child's development so much that other connections in your life have suffered or fallen by the wayside entirely. This is particularly true of parents' partnerships and marriages. Sadly, the number of students who have sought me out in the freshman year in tears because their parents just announced they were separating or divorcing is quite high. The child may well have served as the glue for years. Some parents decided long ago that they would hang in there until the kids left for college, but others fall apart because they suddenly lack the one thing that was holding them together. If this is the case for you, it is not too late. As a first step, take a short walk down memory lane: How did you and your spouse or partner meet? How long was it before you felt love for them? What did you do the first time you spent time together? Was it months or years before you had a child? What was that time like?

As you think back on the very first moments of the love you felt for your spouse, assess how far you have come together. Do you feel more or less or just different affection for them now? Is there work to do to find your way back to each other? Is there a desire to do so? If not, why not? If so, what would be the first step?

It may be very painful to confront the stark differences between the beginnings of your relationship and the present, but evaluating them honestly is a necessary first step toward reanimating things. The second is imagining ways to fix it. It can be as simple as an evening walk hand in hand or reinstituting date night. Or maybe there is so much negativity and pain that counseling is a reasonable next move.

If you are unpartnered at the moment but would like a life partner, you may be about to experience a resurgence of desire coupled with opportunity. It has never been easier to meet people who are looking for love.

Whether you are single or part of a couple, struggling or well-off financially, fit or out of shape, in a rural, suburban, or urban area, thirty-five or seventy years of age, the structure of your days is about to change, and you can choose to use the freed-up time in a million different ways. Planning to do so will make it all the more doable.

Visualizing Your Life After Drop-off

Before you turn the page to move-in, there is one final thing you may want to do: Plan and visualize the goodbye and the first days after drop-off. It will benefit you immeasurably, especially if the thought of your child going to college strikes some fear into your heart. Some people like to do this exercise on paper, others electronically. One particularly artistic mother I worked with even painted it on canvas. Visualizing the moment of farewell and planning the two weeks following move-in will help you put one foot in front of the other once they cross that threshold, whether you drop them off on campus or say goodbye at an airport or bus station.

What Next?

1. Imagine the goodbye. Keep it short, sweet, and loving. Now, what will you do next? Dinner? A luxurious bath? A good, stiff cocktail? Alone? With a significant other? An old friend?
2. Imagine and plan your schedule for the two weeks following move-in.

3. Consider whether your sleep and meal schedules will change now that you don't have to do any or less (by one mouth) meal prep.
4. Note, in particular, where you might have a free hour or two.
5. Planning takes a bit of time. Thinking back on your physical, mental, spiritual, and intellectual health, what positive steps can you take in these two weeks?
6. Regarding your professional and financial life, have you set up new endeavors and appointments? If not, plan to do it now.
7. Thinking of your social and community engagement, which new activities or connections do you want to pursue this fall? Who are the people you haven't seen in a while but would like to? If you haven't done so yet, you can do it now!
8. Finally, when it comes to the all-important family and love relationships, are there people you can spend time with during these two weeks? Which are the most doable and appealing? Which draw you in the most?

Now you are ready!

PART III

Starting Strong

> Midlife is not flyover territory. Midlife is O'Hare,
> midlife is Heathrow, midlife is a bustling hub where the
> decisions you make today largely determine the rest of
> your journey on the planet.
>
> —Barbara Bradley Hagerty, *Life Reimagined*

By this time, you and your child have traversed a great deal of unfamiliar territory, but there is more. While you will be trying to make sure that your kid gets off on the right foot at college, you are grappling to some extent or the other with the daily absence of the teenager who has moved out. Whether you approach the move-in to college with happiness, dread, or a mixture of both, the chapters ahead will lead you through the fall by giving you an understanding of some of the most salient college issues your child will encounter while simultaneously advancing your healthy detachment and helping you actualize an inspired rediscovery of yourself and the important relationships in your life.

At first, everyone feels a bit at sea. Students confront a lot of newness without the daily scaffolding (hopefully!) of their parents, familiar high school structures, and community. For some, being unmoored is not totally unpleasant, so they weather it pretty well. For others, it doesn't go as smoothly. I have watched hundreds of students ignore the unsettling feeling of being at sea until it reached crisis proportions before they asked for help. In many of these cases, students asked so late that they had already done themselves irreparable academic or even physical harm.

As for the parent, this is the time for you to start focusing on you. Recalling what you thought about in the late spring and summer, you can get started on the many aspects of your health, possibly some new professional endeavors, and engaging in new and fun ways in your social and community life. If you are a parent whose heart aches at the thought of your child no longer being at home, this will give you plenty to do during the worst moments. Even if you fall into the category of those who couldn't wait for that moment of freedom from child-rearing, these pages will help direct your newfound autonomy in ways you may not have considered.

CHAPTER 6

September Transitions

As rising freshmen prepare to make the most momentous move of their lives so far, it is helpful for them to know something about culture shock, a process they are about to undergo, whether they like it or not. This is the phase that follows what I call pre–culture shock, discussed in Chapter 3. It comprises a predictable arc of emotional, psychological, and physical phases. Since you, too, will be confronting some newness, you may find this helps you through the inevitable culture shock of adjusting to your new landscape.

Not everyone moves through the phases of culture shock at the same speed. Nor have you gone through them at the same pace every time you have entered a new environment. You may have marched through them quickly when you went to a new school but slowly when you started to work in an unfamiliar organization, or vice versa. It's impossible to predict. An American colleague of mine, for example, adjusted quickly to life in Berlin, Germany, but got stuck in the worst culture shock phase for a seemingly interminable period of time in a small New England town.

You can't know ahead of time how the process will go, but what I call the culture shock cycle has four predictable phases. You might move through them in order, or enter one and go back and forth for a while. If you are aware of them, you can interpret the symptoms your child may be exhibiting, name the phase (if not for them, at least for yourself), assure them that the next one is coming, and help them ask for help when needed.

The culture shock cycle is made up of four basic phases. The first is often called the *honeymoon phase*. This is where your college freshman sees their new environment through the proverbial rose-colored glasses. Every year, students proclaim in ecstatic terms how much they love the campus, the people, their RA and academic advisor, every professor, the subject matter, and the weather. Even the school's dreaded writing requirement seems appealing. This could last a week, a month, or even a whole semester. It's a heady time, when students have boundless energy for the novelty of it all and embrace every aspect of their new lives. They walk around the campus in wonder at their good fortune, and the reports home are gleefully positive. Parents and friends are thrilled that they sound so good and that the adjustment is going so well, confirming that the months of decision-making were well spent. Because they have so much energy, the student signs up for a few different extracurricular activities, puts themselves out there and begins to make lots of friends, does all of their homework, and loses a couple of pounds. Some even have trouble sleeping more than a few hours a night because they are so excited to get up and greet the next day.

However wonderful the honeymoon phase is, it does not last forever. Eventually, things start to grate on their nerves. While they once thought the food was incredibly good, now they start to wonder why. They can't imagine how they ever saw that salad bar as inviting. That bean salad! Ugh! They complain bitterly about their roommate's obvious inability to clean up her side of the room. And why doesn't she ever leave? Doesn't she have any friends? The school-work has mounted up, and they are facing four midterms and a couple of five-page papers. The extracurriculars have started to demand so much time that they have trouble meeting all of their obligations. They are in a state of intense and constant irritation.

This is called *withdrawal*. In it, we begin to objectify everything about the new environment and see it negatively. Students get home-sick beyond belief, and their reports home start sounding grim. They try to maintain a happy tone of voice, but you can hear right through it. They are desperate to get out of there and can't wait to come home for Thanksgiving, so they start inquiring about travel plans. They might have trouble getting up for class, or start spending time by themselves and avoiding their newly established social circles. They cry sometimes and start asking you if they can come home for the weekend soon rather than wait until Thanksgiving.

I didn't know it then, and in fact I didn't realize it for many years, but this is precisely the phase I found myself in when I called my parents sobbing in the third week of the semester, begging to come home. My mother responded by suggesting I wait until Thanksgiving to return. Though I felt like my life was coming to an end, and I just knew I couldn't bear a single day longer at that college, I survived. I did more than that. I began to adjust in a positive and productive way.

That is because withdrawal is usually followed relatively quickly by a third phase, appropriately called *adjustment*. The new place becomes ever-more familiar, and we begin to negotiate it well. Your new college student will now adjust to the amount of work, drop out of an extracurricular or two, and try to figure out which of their new friends are keepers. Their reports home are no longer as elated as they once were, but they also aren't as bleak as they were at the lowest point, either. Your child is more even-keeled. The new campus is feeling a bit more like home. In this period, roommates start agreeing on reasonable guidelines for tidiness and a schedule for spending time alone in the room. In the best of scenarios, freshmen have met with a couple of faculty and advisors and had good conversations about their academic interests and their personal transition. They are quickly moving to the fourth and final stage of culture shock: *independence*. By the time they reach this last phase, they have fully integrated into the new environment, having attained a level of knowledge of and familiarity with the prevailing culture, ethos, and expectations. For your college student, campus is really becoming a home.

Knowing about the predictability of this cycle would have helped Sid during his freshman year at Boston University, five hours from his hometown. The first week on campus, he was elated, happy to experience everything that was so different from home. Being in a city, having been welcomed so many times by faculty, administrators, and older students, organizing his dorm room—all of it had been a tremendous high for him. But quickly, more quickly than for most, the elation turned to utter dread, disgust, and depression. Everything that had seemed bright, new, and wonderful just a week earlier suddenly felt cold, dark, and unwelcoming. He called his mother, sobbing, and demanded to go home. She had never heard him like this before, and it frightened her. She immediately made the drive to Boston, helped him pack up his room, and brought him home, where he spent the rest of the fall working at a fast-food restaurant and trying to figure out what his next step in life would be.

Life Cycles

- Think about your child's life transitions. How was their move from elementary school to middle school? Middle school to high school?
- How did they adjust to new organizations or teams they joined? How quickly did they recognize the prevailing culture and adjust to it?

- Have they ever moved from one town to another? How did that go?
- In any of the transitions in their lives, can you recognize the phases of the culture shock cycle?

When your child begins to enter the predictable phases of culture shock, the desire to swoop in and save them can become intense. For many students, as for Sid (and for me), there comes a moment in the first weeks of college when they desperately want to withdraw from school and race home. They panic, and so do their parents. Some students go home and never return. If they had only known that they were experiencing a predictable phase in the college adjustment cycle, they could have accessed the plentiful support resources on campus and weathered the crisis productively.

The Countless Sources of Support

How in the world are they going to deal with all this—the absence of parents, the lack of a surefire path, the seeming structurelessness of the days, weeks, and months, the vast diversity of thoughts, beliefs, cultures, and mores they will encounter, and the culture shock they will experience? Luckily, students never have to go it alone.

Campuses hire hundreds if not thousands of people who have made a conscious decision to spend their professional lives at an institution of higher education. As mentioned in Chapter 2, everyone from the maintenance workers, dining hall employees, and grounds-keepers to the administrative assistants, advisors, teachers, and healthcare staff has made a personal choice to seek employment at this college and to pursue a career that gives them the opportunity to interact with people who value the academic enterprise. Few people seek employment at a college as a default or because they have no other choice. In fact, securing a job at a college or university is usually not easy. Because these institutions are known to be such great employers, job searches can be quite competitive.

Why is this important to you as a new college parent? Because each and every person your child meets on a campus is potentially interested in them as a human being and wants to see them succeed. (Some will be more interested in them than others, of course.) Unfortunately, the overwhelming majority of college students miss out on the opportunity to utilize this vast network of potential support. But when asked, college employees stand ready, willing, and able to invest in them, to guide them, to share a story, or even just to offer a smile when they are down.

One of the main jobs of a college student should be to cultivate relationships with professors, lecturers, graduate students, administrators, librarians, dining services employees, janitors, and everyone else they come across on campus. In doing so, they can build their own rich community of advisors, friends, and acquaintances. Some students become so close to the maintenance staff in their dorms that they take up a collection before the holidays and present them with a gift before they leave for winter break! Any adult on campus is a prospective source of wisdom and advice. The relationships they develop with them may be very different from the relationships they have had with adults up to this point. This is something to embrace.

The sad truth, however, is that most students complete college without taking advantage of the caring faculty and staff on their campus. Why? It's simple, really. They get absorbed in making friends. Cultivating those relationships seems paramount. It's easy to ignore the wealth of older, more experienced, and often wiser people who are virtually everywhere in their new community. Faculty and staff may spend decades on a campus and have a lot of insight and advice to offer. While undergraduates experience their college for just a few semesters, they often give their peers' opinions a great deal of credibility and never think to ask the adults who dedicate their lives to that institution. This is a missed opportunity.

What Most Students Miss Out On: Connecting with Faculty

This is a good moment to help your child prepare to get to know faculty, something that will make an enormous difference in the college experience. Most college and university employees sadly take it as a given that the majority of faculty sit alone in their offices during weekly office hours without a single undergraduate visitor. This means that students are missing out on an invaluable chance to do something that could enhance their intellectual and academic experience immeasurably: Get to know faculty.

Why does research confirm time and time again that connecting with faculty in a substantive way is so beneficial? Here are a few reasons:

1. Talking to faculty about course material deepens the student's knowledge of the field and course.
2. The conversations can give students a more concise idea of what is important from the instructor's perspective, which enables them to tailor study time more efficiently.
3. Consulting with faculty about paper topics and other written exercises improves one's research, the writing process, and the final product.
4. Attending office hours signals interest in the course, never a bad thing.
5. Once faculty members know a student's name and have a sense of their engagement in the course material, they may call on them in class more often.
6. Students gain more comfort contributing to class discussion, thus deepening their knowledge of the subject and increasing the participation grade.
7. Investment in the topic may inspire them to lead a study group, which will not only enhance their grasp of the material but look good on their résumé.

8. Conversations with faculty may lead to a solid paper topic or even guide the choice of major, concentration, minor, programs, certificates, and so on.

9. Many students find out about research opportunities and receive invaluable career advice during these meetings.

10. Students spend four years on campus; faculty spend a lifetime. They have wisdom and knowledge to share. Undergraduates are young and don't know much yet; instructors are older and know a lot more.

11. And, to be even more mercenary about it, students might be able to ask that faculty member for a *good* letter of recommendation down the road, one that will catapult them to the top of the pile of applicants for important internships, fellowships, or scholarships.

Years ago I met a brilliant student named Tom. We have kept in touch over the years, and I have had the great fortune to meet his parents and siblings. I count his mother among my friends, in fact. When I asked Tom what he wishes he had known before he started college, he wrote: "I was lucky to have taken several small seminar courses in my first two years, which means that I formed relationships with my professors. Left to my own devices in a larger lecture class, I would have been too intimidated to make myself known to them. But those relationships made my experience so much better. They felt comfortable writing about me when I asked for recommendations for fellowships, and I was exposed to other seminar classes that they offered. Plus, they are a resource for you throughout your time in college and beyond. I still ask my professors for career advice. I still pester my academic advisor with emails. She encouraged me to reach out and maintain relationships, and I think that was great advice."

It sounds so simple: Get to know faculty! But most students feel completely intimidated at the prospect of approaching a professor, so here are a few words on how they should go about it.

1. Before visiting, they should find out the office hours (usually posted on a website or available through the departmental administrator), find a day and time that fits into their schedule, and send the professor an email saying they plan to come. (If they have schedule conflicts, they can always email the professor to set up a time outside of office hours.)

2. Before going, they need to read the instructor's webpages and note where they went to college and graduate school and what the titles of their books and articles are. How do they describe themselves in their bio? Is their CV (curriculum vitae, the academic brand of résumé) posted? Reading around on the website not only helps them prep for the meeting but teaches them something about the field.

3. Then they need only draft two to three questions about the course, the readings, the at-home work, or other relevant matters. These should not be on the order of "What should I write about?" Rather, "I'm thinking of writing about X. I found the topic so interesting. Do you have suggestions for how I should go about approaching that? Are there other texts I should consult?" These conversations are the perfect venue for being honest about academic struggles, maybe something like "I'm struggling with my writing. Do you have any advice?" "What advice do you have for a new undergraduate at this school?" Faculty are no strangers to these sorts of things.

4. Faculty usually appreciate interest in them as scholars as well, so asking them about their research is a good idea, too. "How did you get interested in this area of inquiry?" "Did you always want to be a professor of XYZ?"

5. Students should dress appropriately (i.e., cover body parts like cleavage, belly buttons, and underclothing; not wear a baseball cap or other casual attire; et cetera), sit up, be respectful, and address them as "Professor [insert last name]" unless they have been instructed otherwise.

6. Finally, they should send them an email of thanks: "Dear Pro-

fessor [insert last name], I really appreciated your time today, and I felt I learned a great deal about X, Y, and Z. I look forward to your next class. Sincerely, [student's full name, course number and title]."

The following are a couple of great examples of students who benefited from forming secure and strong attachments to adults on campus, whether they were advisors, faculty, adjuncts, graduate students, principal investigators in a science lab, work-study supervisors, or administrative assistants. These show that sources of advice and support, both formal and informal, are thick on the ground at every college.

Danielle, one of four children raised by a single mom, attended an Ivy for undergrad and then Harvard Law School. She worked for one of the most prestigious law firms in the country and then did a clerkship with a federal judge. When I asked her what she wished she had known before she went to college, one of the things she wrote was: "I wish I would've sought out the support of older students, or grad students, or adults who got it. I was fortunate enough to have a dean at my residential college who sought me out, checked in with me, gave me advice, and provided much-needed perspective (which no one under the age of twenty-five has). . . . And I should've confided in her about personal in addition to academic topics. She would've told me straight, and I wouldn't have suffered [so much] if I'd had more guiding lights around me in a sea of absolute darkness."

The relationships formed with adults on campus may differ considerably from those your child has had in the past. Especially if they connect substantively with someone who will not grade them in a course, the relationship is one of pure interest in them as a human being. The adults who work on campus are not generally interested in judging; they merely want to help students figure out the next steps in their lives. Being open to getting to know these people can benefit them, in both the short and long term. They can turn to them for help on any given day, use them as a sounding board, check their understanding of random things, and perhaps even get letters of recommendation from them for an internship or job.

Gary came from a wealthy New England family and had gone to a posh prep school before arriving at his college. He knew he would follow in his father's footsteps and assume leadership of the family investment firm sometime in the future, so he didn't have any worries or concerns about his position in life or his ability to make a living. But he had instinctively always felt drawn to adults, and he looked forward to establishing close relationships with some at college. When he met his first advisor, he took an immediate dislike to her. She seemed cold and judgmental. He was so disappointed. So he went to the dean in charge of the advising office and asked if he could be assigned to a new advisor. After ten or fifteen minutes of talking, Gary was so comfortable with her that he asked if she would advise him. She said she would be happy to. For the next four years, Gary went by about once a month to talk. Only once did he have a true crisis—a disciplinary hearing due to a fistfight in town—and she was helpful then. But mostly he just wanted to talk about his life, courses, direction in life, fraternity activities, friends, and other relationships. Staying close to his advisor served as a personal gauge for him of how much he was changing and growing. And it was a true source of comfort. When he graduated, he and his family took the dean out to a very fancy lunch to thank her for all of the help and guidance. The advisor was pleased that it had meant so much to them. She had enjoyed the conversations and time with Gary as much as he had enjoyed them. Gary was also able to get a detailed and substantive letter of recommendation from her for his graduate school application.

Obviously, the strong attachment Gary had to his advisor served him as a scaffolding of sorts during his years at college. The dean only had his best interests at heart. She wanted to support him whenever he needed it. This is the purest form of student/advisor relationship. Of course, Gary and the dean talked about requirements, rules, regulations, and responsibilities, but those did not form the basis of the attachment. It was the selfless, nonjudgmental support she provided that made the difference for Gary. If every college student had at least one such relationship with an adult on their campus, the college experience would be exponentially enhanced for everyone.

Students will come across caring individuals in research labs, academic departments, and work-study jobs. They will meet them in discussion sections, at language tables, and at talks. Librarians, dining hall employees, custodians, gardeners, departmental administrators, finance and financial aid people, admission officers, registrar staff, facilities folks, and everyone else on a campus is a potential source of care, understanding, and warmth.

I'll say it once again: Regardless of whether or not they have obvious needs for particular types of support on campus, students do themselves a service by seeking out and cultivating strong attachments to several adults who are on the college payroll. Chances are that they are committed to the well-being and success of every student who crosses their paths.

The reason I highlight this is that the need to develop multiple connections on campus points to an unsettling fact about college that I discussed earlier. No one can find all of the answers to all of their questions in one place. In high school, students pretty much knew exactly where to go for help or advice, and it was usually their parents, friends, a guidance counselor, a favorite teacher, or a coach. Though new students often expect the advisor assigned to them in their first year to know all of the answers, college advising is never a one-stop-shopping experience. There is one other unhappy truth: You may ask one person a question about a given course, organization, or major and get one answer, and then get a completely different response from the next person. Why? Because colleges and especially universities are big, intricate places. No one knows everything about them, and everyone experiences them from their own vantage point. Faculty members, administrators, librarians, dining services employees—they all have opinions of the place, because each of them spends the day in their own corners. Of course their perspectives differ. To make things even more opaque, the college equivalents of urban legends are everywhere, and they are often wrong and always tough to dispel. This can be troubling until students learn to use these conflicting pieces of advice to their advantage.

A freshman I once knew named Charles arrived on campus eager to figure out which creative writing classes to choose. Then he heard from students he talked to that it was virtually impossible to get into one as a first-year student. He was completely devastated. He also heard really bad things about the most famous poet on the faculty. Charles was distraught and thought he had made the wrong decision to come to that school. When he met with his advisor to discuss this awful turn of events, she asked him if she could see some of his poetry. He pulled some tattered papers out of his bag. As she read through the pages, she realized this was a talented, already fairly advanced poet. She called the creative writing department and asked if there were seats for freshmen in the famous poet's course. The administrator said he should come right over, and she would see what she could do. Charles met with her and then with the poet himself and was admitted to his fall seminar. Contrary to everything horrible he had heard about this poet from his peers, Charles found the poet accessible, gracious, and encouraging, and they entered into what would become a decades-long mentoring relationship.

The obvious moral of this story is that it's absolutely essential that students resist listening to the ubiquitous chatter and make their own decisions about every professor, advisor, course, major, and activity. To believe others rather than figure it out on their own denies them their individuality and autonomy. College is going to offer them a degree of self-sufficiency that may be new to them. If they are not practiced in what I call "self-guidedness," then this may be overwhelming. It is our nature that encourages us to join the pack, to avoiding sticking out, to blend right in with our peers, and to hold the same opinions of everything from clothing to food to other people. For freshmen, though, it is time to resist the herding impulse and start thinking independently. This is easier said than done, as the pull of peers is strong. But obviously, first-year students are trying to forge their own unique path, one that reflects who they are, so they need to listen to themselves to make their college experience and build foundations for career development that speak to their individuality.

That's why the single most important thing they can do (other than their assigned schoolwork, of course), as mentioned in Chapter 2, is to get to know lots of faculty and staff members and build their own board or community of advisors. As adults, when we move to a new community, we seek out the best doctors, dentists, grocers, gyms, butchers, accountants, religious communities, and schools, just to name a few. We find them by asking people in the know, those who have lived in the community for years. We often get conflicting advice, but we use the initial advice to check them all out and decide for ourselves which ones suit us best. This is exactly the situation for new students in college. Their natural tendency is to look to their peers for advice, but other undergraduates have only been on campus one to three years. That's nothing compared to the decades faculty and administrators dedicate to the place, so they should seek out people who have been there for a while and ask them for their opinions and insights on everything from soup to nuts: courses, majors, activities, sights in the area, banks, restaurants, and parks. Then they need to check them out for themselves.

Remind Your New College Student

- Sources of support on campus are thick on the ground.
- Every college has faculty and administrators who dedicate decades of their lives to that institution. Seeking them out will enrich the college experience.

- Every student should begin building their own community of advisors, since college is never a one-stop advising experience. Everyone has their own opinions, and students can use the information they gather from various corners to make up their own mind about courses, professors, and everything else.

What Do You Still Have to Do with It?

Now more than ever before, your contribution to your child's college experience will be essential. Whether faculty and administrators like it or not (and many really can't stand it), the ways you support your son or daughter in the coming four years will have a decisive impact on their ability to complete the degree and their first steps after graduation. While some people still argue forcefully that you just have to kick them out of that nest and let them fly, I maintain that that philosophy belongs to a bygone era, when your kid's room could be counted on for another purpose once they flew the coop at eighteen years of age.

When I moved into my dorm, my parents barely slowed the car down, and they didn't let me come home until Thanksgiving. They held the popular belief that cutting the cord completely at the moment college began was the right way to do things. They thought they would have done me a great disservice if they hadn't severed their daily support from day one. But things are radically different now. Students who have the steady support of their parents are more likely to get a degree on time and secure a seat in graduate school or a position in the world of work directly after graduation.

Additionally, there are two practical facts that make continuous parental engagement with their college-age children not just a good idea but almost a necessity. As already mentioned, 80 percent of positions in the United States are gotten through connections. And an equal percentage of job openings in U.S. organizations are never advertised. They are in the so-called hidden job market. That means that parents can play a decisive role in helping kids get connected, both on campus and off, in whatever industries are of interest.

For on-campus networking, you can help your college-age children research faculty and administrators and encourage them to connect with them. That will help ensure they make ample use of the academic and career advising resources available to them from day one. You may also be able to attend parent and family events, either in person in your area or remotely, where you can get to know faculty, administrators, and other parents.

In off-campus networking, you can play a decisive role as well. If you are in the pharmaceutical industry and your child wants to be an actor, you might wonder how that would work. Or say you are a car mechanic and your daughter's dream is to go to medical school. No matter how far apart your actual and their potential professions are, you can lend a hand. By talking to people in all of your circles about their personal and professional networks, you can connect your child with the friend of a friend of a colleague. Or you can work your LinkedIn profile and professional organizations and engage with people at your place of worship or in civic associations, even if you only have tenuous connections to them. Even when shopping at your local grocery store or perusing books at your library, you may strike up a conversation with someone who knows someone who . . .

Take the example of Noah. His mom was a college administrator and his dad a professional musician in New York City. Noah chose to study business in college with the goal of becoming a real estate agent in the countryside, somewhere north of the city. Neither parent had any connection whatsoever to business or real estate, and they never had the money to buy a home. They were mystified by the idea that they could ever connect Noah to anyone who could help, but they started talking to colleagues at work and acquaintances at their temple and eventually found people open to giving Noah an informational interview. Noah begrudgingly listened to the advice that he should never leave one of those conversations without the names of at least two other connections, so his network grew quickly. By the time he finished college, not only had he had four fantastic internships that helped him identify what he liked and didn't like in the profession, but he had a job offer to boot two hours north of home.

The nation's universities and colleges are still grappling with the question of the best and most appropriate ways to engage parents, guardians, and families in the college experience of their undergraduates (and even their graduate students). As they have struggled to find the right balance, their philosophies on family engagement have evolved a lot, as have the services they offer. It used to be a given that drop-off was the watershed moment, and that parents disappeared until graduation. Now, though, parents' assumed absence has been replaced with continuous presence. But, still, not all colleges welcome the involvement.

On the face of it, the ways in which parents and extended families are welcomed on a college campus may seem trivial. But it's interesting to note that, because of the unabating trend of increasing parental involvement in the lives of their college-age children, over 50 percent of the colleges that now have parent and family program offices have opened them in the past fifteen years or so. Saying they engage parents and actually doing it are two different things. The services colleges offer vary a lot, from a single webpage and online handbook to large orientation events and elaborate support and engagement structures.

Colleges that are ahead of the curve are engaging parents in lots of productive ways. They ask them to organize parent gatherings in their areas, invite them to online talks, allow them to enroll in courses designed for community members, and solicit internship opportunities for current students or approach moms and dads about considering new alumni in their firm's applicant pools. Colleges have also come to rely on parental donations for a portion of their operating and financial aid budgets, so their development offices may set up parent councils ostensibly to advise the deans and others even as high up as the president. These invitations are typically extended to the well-heeled, who are later pressured to write big checks so that the college can reach its fundraising targets.

It's no secret that the children of potentially big donors are the "special-interest students" whose impending presence is announced to the president, deans, advisors, housing staff, and others who will interact with them. I wouldn't go so far as to say that these kids are treated differently in every respect; in fact, many institutions will go out of their way to act as if they are not special at all. But the truth is that exceptions are often made for them. Administrators talk about them in code, and decisions are swayed based on their status as financial lifelines and as potential subjects of media attention. No college wants to be in the headlines for housing a celebrity's child in a vermin-ridden dorm or failing them in any way in the slightest. Before their arrival, development staff will typically give lists of special-interest families to housing and advising to make sure that a relatively good dorm is chosen and the kid will get into classes. Whether they are kings, princesses, scions of global conglomerates, or—my favorite from years ago—an arms dealer in the Middle East, their children will probably get the white-glove treatment. Rooms and course selection are the first but certainly not the last accommodations made for them. The final ones will be great seating at graduation followed by fancier receptions and meals to celebrate the occasion with the college president, deans, faculty, and other luminaries.

Let's get back to the parent and family office. Often, the employees who lead these offices have enormous job portfolios in addition to parental support. And they are usually not well compensated, even though they are accountable at high levels. What does that mean? For example, when a parent sends an email to the university president complaining about bad advising or poor course options or mice in the dorm, the president's office will immediately forward the complaint to the family support office to compose a response. So it is helpful to remember that parent and family programs employees have a great deal of responsibility, work hard, and are typically earning less—much less—than you think.

Let's take a look at a couple of college offices that support parents to get a sense of the variety. At this writing, Macalester College in Minnesota offers the following to parents:

- Website
- Handbook
- Parent Council
- Volunteer opportunity sign-up
- FAQs and tips
- Newsletter

The webpages are hosted by the Office of Student Affairs, but the contact info for a person responsible for the support of parents and families is elusive. This probably means that a number of student affairs professionals are co-leading the various activities surrounding families, and that they have lots of other work to do as well. Or it could mean that a job search is under way.

At Emory College in Atlanta, the Office of Parent and Family Programs is led by an assistant vice president in charge of both alumni relations and parent and family programs. The title means that this person directs the offices that engage with both alumni and the parents of current students. That is a gigantic portfolio, but an increasingly common structure. The Emory office has a robust suite of offerings, including newsletters, family weekends, webinars, family panels, and receptions in various cities just for families. Even more impressive, Emory has a list of useful contacts that includes people's names, titles, and phone numbers. Colleges often hide the names of people responsible for parents for various reasons. Sometimes it means that they really do not want direct contact from parents. But most often it means that a number of people are shouldering the work while also having the equivalent of a full-time job serving students, and they do not want any one person overburdened by parents and their many and unpredictable needs and requests. Most staffing structures and budgets have just not caught up to the expectations of today's parents. At other institutions, it could be a sign of ambivalence or even a negative stance toward parental presence on the campus.

Often parents look for support and information outside of the college. And luckily, resources abound. Their "mission is to assist families in the successful preparation, transition, adjustment, and completion through college," as College Parents of America notes. College Parent Central (collegeparentcentral.com), which came into being only a few years ago, lists many other helpful websites and books. In fact, the reasons that some colleges hold a less-than-welcoming perspective toward parents become clear when we turn our attention to the five tenets listed on College Parent Central:

- "We believe that parents *are partners* in their child's education from pre-school through college.
- We believe that parents *want to be involved* in their child's college experience.
- We believe that parents *have a place* in their child's college experience.
- We believe that many parents *are unsure how* to be involved in their child's college experience.
- We believe that many parents *need to better understand* college today in order to support their student."

While these statements might sound completely reasonable to you, they send shudders down the spines of many faculty and administrators. Many object vehemently to such tenets because they believe that parents should not partner with their children in the college experience. At all. Or that the college should not partner with the parent. In fact, they still believe, as my parents did, that parents should be absent from day one. Yes, even though the parents are often footing the bill and research shows that they have a hand in successful and timely degree completion, some colleges still go to great lengths to exclude parents, trusting that children are best able to develop into adults if they break the cord as soon as they step onto campus.

Regardless of the college's stance on parents, what you need to know first and foremost is whom you can call if you have a concern or question. It is natural for you to think of reaching out to RAs, especially if you met them during move-in. But parental inquiries put the RA in a tough spot. They are, after all, just students, slightly older peers of your child. In their extensive training program, there was definitely a whole session dedicated to ways of handling parents. Expect the response to your questions to RAs to be something like "Shall I ask your son/daughter to call you?" or "Let me put you in touch with the right person for that issue, okay?"

Residential life is organized hierarchically. The RAs are described as the "front line." Over them there could be four or five tiers of ever-more extensively trained and experienced professionals, be they graduate students, faculty, or administrators, who handle everything from roommate conflicts to ladybug infestations to outbreaks of salmonella, not to mention drug abuse, crime, and other health and safety issues.

As a parent, I would rarely if ever reach out to the RA. It could be embarrassing to your child, and it will always have an impact on the RA's relationship with them. How could it not? You do not want to be "that parent." All you have to do is find out who the right adults on campus are for your questions and concerns.

A stellar example of a well-staffed parent relations office can be found at Gettysburg College in Pennsylvania. With an undergraduate student body of only 2,500 students, the college has dedicated three full-time people to parents. That is truly impressive, especially given the budgetary constraints most colleges face these days. Gettysburg is a college that, by the looks of it, has decided to prioritize parents and embrace them 100 percent. That is a beneficial stance for many reasons, the most important of which is, as already stated, that when colleges partner productively with parents to support students, it is more likely that an undergraduate will finish a degree on time. In other words, engaging parents can be, as we call it in the world of higher ed, an effective institutional retention strategy. Retaining students means being able to count on their tuition and future donations, so college investment in parent and family offices and events pays off big-time.

Here is a sampling of parental inquiries college offices may field in a given year:

- I need to replace the linoleum in my son's room with natural wood. When can I send the workmen in?
- Would you have someone wake up my daughter every morning before class begins? She hits the snooze button a lot.
- Rob can't get into the chemistry lab that doesn't conflict with his internship. Who can fix that?
- There are ladybugs/mice/roaches/bedbugs in the dorm. My child needs to move immediately.
- Tony got an F in Economics 101, which will ruin his life. What's the process for getting that removed?
- Sally needs to attend a family reunion during orientation, so she will arrive on campus late. How can she make up what she will miss?
- I haven't heard from Tim in over twenty-four hours. We've never gone this long without communicating before. Can you find him and see if he's okay?
- Mario will get sick if he can't have my bone marrow soup every week. We know hotplates aren't permitted, but we need an exception so he can have one in his room.
- Final exams end on December 23, but our family leaves for Europe on the twenty-first, so we need to move the exams up for Sissy. (Not usually possible. Even for a family trip!)
- Your career education/academic advising/dorm room/dining hall is terrible. Why am I paying all this money?

- I need someone to lay out Jimmy's meds every morning.
- Sue needs a home cleaning/laundry service. Whom do you recommend?
- My son's roommate is gay/transgender/straight/not white/not black/a foreigner/strange/wealthy/not wealthy/fat/anorexic. He needs to move.
- My daughter's roommates are stealing her food. I demand restitution, and she needs to move ASAP.
- My son is allergic to Lysol, and his roommates won't stop spraying it in the bathroom.
- The toilets clog up daily.
- Who is cleaning the bathrooms? They are filthy.
- Professor X is boring. My kid can't learn from him.
- The RA told my son to send his samurai sword back home. What could you possibly have against a work of art like that?

Not all of these are reasons for parents to reach out. In fact, not one of them is! If you find yourself heading for the phone in cases like those, stop yourself now.

So, then, what are the best and most sensible reasons to reach out to these folks? Those fall into three categories. The first is that you are seriously concerned about your child's well-being. Every college wants to know when a student is exhibiting telltale signs of high stress levels that could have an impact on their ability to meet the demands of daily life at college. Parents are still often the first to detect changes in their child's behavior or demeanor. The parent and family office, or whoever is designated to receive such information, should welcome it and follow up immediately using their well-established protocols.

The second reason to reach out to them is to get information that you can't find on the website but need in order to help advise or encourage your child when she is struggling with a given task, such as registration, dining plans, conflicts with someone on campus, completing coursework, meeting deadlines, researching and writing papers, finding the right social/civic engagement opportunities, and so on. The purpose of your email or phone call will be to gain an understanding of the resources or options available to a student so that you can inform your child about various ways to meet the challenge she is facing.

The third motivation for contacting them is to offer to enrich the life of the college in some way. You may want to host a wine and cheese event for other parents in your area, or provide some insights in an upcoming webinar, or advertise a job or internship. Any attempt on your part to contribute to the community will most likely be welcome.

It's Your Turn!

Knowing that your child has infinite support mechanisms hopefully makes it easier for you to turn your attention to yourself. Remember the thoughts you had and plans you put in place in the spring and summer? It's time to execute!

The point is not to imagine a life that involves not caring for your child. Even if you've just dropped off your youngest child at college, you know that your parenting is not over. Far from it. Your child needs your help to make the transition well and get to the degree on time. But you are now able to take some of the time and physical and mental energy you have dedicated on a daily, weekly, and monthly basis to your children and reroute it to something else. How exciting and fortunate you are! Some parents experience gnawing guilt at this thought. If you are one of them, take comfort in the idea that you are modeling healthy adulthood by continually expanding and stretching yourself, trying new things, and making the most of your moments on this planet. Your child will be proud of you for it, and you will undoubtedly feel intense gratification as you execute the next steps in the process. Other parents feel guilty because they can't wait to start enjoying themselves in new ways and diving into new adventures. Don't waste time on negative emotions. Just enjoy your new-found freedom. You've earned it.

Dream, Imagine, Plan

This fall is your time to act expansively and imaginatively.

- What's the most productive and fun thing you can do to augment your physical health?
- Are there mental barriers to reaching imagined goals?
- Does your spiritual life need a lift?
- Are there intellectual pathways you are intrigued by?

Enhancing your life is exciting. It has the added benefit of modeling for your child the beauty of always being able to grow and consider priorities anew.

Your process of opening yourself up to new things parallels your child's experience. As you search for and find new things that make life gratifying, productive, and fun, your new college student is doing the same. This simultaneous practice offers both of you a new way to connect and stay close, even at a geographical distance from each other.

CHAPTER 7

Fall Encounters

Every parent knows that part of acclimating to college is their child's inescapable experiences with religious, political, racial, ethnic, socioeconomic, and drug-, alcohol-, sex-, and gender-related differences that are new and sometimes surprising. Especially in this age of widespread social activism, this can be terrifying and anxiety-provoking for everyone involved.

When they finally arrive on campus, the first thing students encounter is diversity like they've probably never seen before. Even though their high school may have had a rainbow of differences, your student had four years to get used to them, and by the time graduation rolled around, everyone was probably pretty familiar. Now they are starting over again, and in almost all cases, the pool of newness and difference is at a whole different scale. From the very first day, they meet people who have different religious beliefs, political preferences, cultural practices, and social, ethical, and moral standards. It can be jarring to hear peers espouse views that are 180 degrees apart from their own. After all, they seem to have so much in common: age, choice of school, global icons, social media preferences, and popular culture. They often assume they will share more than they do with other college students. Certainly they will find some who hold ideas that are close to their own at some point, but they will also be in close contact with people who hold views they may find surprising and thought-provoking, at times delightful, and at others even repugnant.

It is true and not surprising that young people often need guidance to learn how to make the best of difference. For this reason, it is useful to find out what sorts of educational opportunities and services regarding diversity are available on your child's campus. If enabling students to learn how to work and live with people who differ from them is a priority at the college, as it is at most, there will be multiple chances for all students to engage in educational diversity programs. These can be exceptionally valuable even though most students approach them like they do a dental appointment. Substantive support and guidance by the college ensure that chances to learn from one another are not squandered.

Ideally, you have instilled in your child the necessity of approaching each encounter with difference, no matter what kind, with politeness, openness, and respect. And your child surely knows intellectually how important this is. But it can be easier said than done when hundreds or thousands of eighteen- to twenty-two-year-olds find themselves in an unfamiliar environment meeting people rapidly in one venue after another while feeling extraordinary pressure to be happy, have fun, make friends, and be productive. At some point, constant dissimilarity wears on all of us, and we will seek out the comfort of familiarity for a brief respite. If your child finds himself in need of a break and can't find someone who offers them that on campus, suggest that they reach out to family and friends from home. Their high school friends have started new lives, too, and are probably in need of a friendly voice as well.

Imagine the following scenarios:

- A devout Christian is assigned to room with a student who can't wait to get to college so that she can come out of the closet.
- An observant Jew and an observant Sunni Muslim are living together.
- A first-generation college student rooms with a fourth-generation legacy.
- Three affluent students have a suitemate from an impoverished background.
- A lacrosse player perceives his roommate to be a dweeby computer scientist.
- A conservative Republican is sharing a room with a politically active anarchist.
- A vegan animal rights activist lives with a meat-and-potatoes lover.

Let's say your child complains to you about something like one of these. What advice would you give them? What resources would you point them to for assistance? I have witnessed every one of these. But students rarely have the foggiest idea where to turn for help in an uncomfortable and unpleasant situation that they can't immediately resolve! Luckily, RAs are trained extensively to help. Above them on the totem pole, there are several layers of even better-trained professionals—graduate students and administrators—who have loads of experience. In fact, their training programs have included scenarios just like these, so they are practiced in facilitating resolutions to even the thorniest issues. Academic advisors are another possible option; they have probably helped students in a situation like this as well.

If you have an inkling that your child or their new acquaintances might be confronting difference that is causing discomfort or concern, urge them to reach out to any one of these people to talk about it. As long as a situation doesn't get out of hand quickly, conversation is the single best way for them to arrive at a solution and to start learning about the process of coping with, learning from, and even appreciating stark differences. If, on the other hand, things spiral out of control, you should not hesitate to contact someone in Student Affairs (sometimes now called Student Success) immediately to make them aware of the need for someone to step in and help.

The Infamous College Partying

One of the most prominent ways that difference most pointedly appears is in the diversity of practices in and attitudes toward alcohol and other drugs and sex. Every campus will inevitably have students with no experience and others with a great deal. This may worry you deeply, confirm what you already suspected, or both, but the National Institute on Alcohol Abuse and Alcoholism estimates that 80 percent of students drink alcohol while at college, and half of those engage in binge-drinking at some point. The institute goes on to state that virtually every college student is affected by drinking, whether they themselves drink or not. That's because regardless of whether a given student drinks or not, they will observe drunken students in the dorms at night, be awakened in the middle of the night by overimbibing peers, and have classes with people who are falling asleep because they are hungover. They might also notice students sneaking alcohol into the dorms and decorating their rooms with the empty bottles as if they were trophies. They will likely know someone who struggles with alcohol addiction and has to leave college for a period of time. Alcohol is ubiquitous, even on dry campuses.

The same goes for other drugs. The use and abuse of prescription pills have become so normalized on college campuses that it is not unusual for the names of the students who sell Adderall, OxyContin, Ritalin, Klonopin, Valium, and Xanax to be common knowledge. Your child will undoubtedly hear about gatherings held expressly for the purpose of exchanging them. Likewise, marijuana, cocaine, ecstasy, and heroin are easy to find on virtually any campus in the

United States. Every year brings new stories of expulsion because of buying or selling drugs; too often we hear of injury or death due to experimentation gone wrong.

What's a parent to do in the face of all this? Right now, the most important thing you can do is to engage your child in conversation about their attitudes toward alcohol, others' prescriptions, and illegal drugs. Have they ever drunk alcohol to excess? Have they taken prescription drugs they got from a friend or seller? Have they taken illegal drugs? Do they plan to drink or take drugs in college? How do they feel about people who have different views regarding these substances? Getting them talking about these important issues is the best way to help them be thoughtful about the decisions they will be asked to make—to partake or not, for starters—when they are away at school.

Besides the physical risk involved in drinking and drugging, your child ought to be aware of the possible disciplinary ramifications of an overly ebullient night. Examples are everywhere in the news. A few years ago, there was a famous case dubbed by law enforcement "Operation Ivy League" in which five students were arrested along with six non-students for peddling drugs on campus, among them Adderall. It turned out that just about every student on campus knew who was selling those tempting little pills in the libraries and dorms.

Since selling prescription drugs is a felony, any student who is caught is typically advised to take a leave of absence right away so that they can tend to legal matters. If they don't, the college will likely suspend them on an interim basis until the court case is settled. If the student states an intention to reenroll after the criminal proceedings conclude, the judicial affairs officers will finally hear their case. If the evidence against them is solid, expulsion would not be an unusual outcome. They will have lost their chance to earn a degree at that institution altogether.

I wish that every student would tuck into the back of their minds the fact that sharing, trading, and selling prescription drugs and trading, selling, and taking illegal drugs may have serious consequences—not only in the courts but also at the university itself. The criminal and college disciplinary proceedings are two separate and distinct processes that do not intersect. In fact, the reason most students are advised to go on a leave of absence if they are caught by law enforcement is so that when the university is subpoenaed for the records for use in the legal proceedings, there won't be any. That is a way of protecting the student from others getting their hands on whatever the college learns during their own investigations.

I highlight this issue because the exchange of prescription drugs, in particular, is so common that students do not realize the gravity of it. These are federal offenses. Committing a crime while at college is never a good idea, but students do it every day without being aware that this one act could destroy their lives in so many ways, in both the short and long term. They may lose their chance to get a degree at that institution and many others. If they are convicted, on every future job and school application they will have to respond "yes" to the question of whether or not they have committed a crime. If the student does get to finish college and then wants to go on to law or medical school, the graduate school will ask the applicant for access to their undergraduate judicial records. Serious offenses may play a decisive role in whether or not you gain admission to the graduate school of your choice. Not to mention the possibility of jail time.

There is yet another variant of the prescription drug issue that occurs with some frequency on campuses as well. Some entering students decide to stop taking their prescribed medication when they arrive as a way of breaking with the past and starting anew, declaring freedom from strictures, or returning to a perhaps idealized state of mind they had access to before they went on medication. Often teenagers resent or dislike being medicated and see college as a chance to be free of it. As adults, we know we should only stop taking medication under the supervision of a medical professional, preferably one who is familiar with our history, diagnosis, and treatment. But for the eighteen-year-old, the urge to liberate oneself from medication can be alluring.

Erin, for instance, had been diagnosed with bipolar disorder in high school. Like Leslie, whose story I told in Chapter 5, she couldn't wait to get to college and go off the many prescription drugs she had been on for three years. She missed the highs, which gave her tons of energy and creativity. She wanted to major in fine arts and felt that the medications would dampen her creativity. She was also sure she was a lot more fun when she wasn't medicated. Once she set foot on campus, she didn't even open her pill bottles. Two weeks into the fall semester, Erin woke up on the side of the road near campus, without any recollection of how she got there. She knew she was hurt, but couldn't tell immediately how badly. Her handbag was gone, so she couldn't call anyone. She began the long walk into town when a car stopped to ask her if she wanted a ride. The driver was a faculty member she recognized, so she got in. The professor insisted on taking her to the hospital, since she was bleeding on both arms and one leg. The hospital called the on-call person at the college, who made the decision to call Erin's parents. They immediately flew out to tend to her.

Erin had fortunately not been sexually assaulted, and her wounds were only superficial, but the psychological impact of the experience did not leave her as quickly as the cuts healed. Plus she had to restart her meds, which took weeks to take effect. In the meantime, she didn't feel well. And her parents lost trust in her ability to live away from home. Her freshman year got off to a very rocky start, emotionally, physically, and academically.

If your child is on medication and you think that they might experiment with tapering off or going cold turkey at college, you may want to check in with them more often than others (this is yet another reason to set up a communication plan before your child leaves home—see Chapter 5). If your child runs into someone who has decided to go off their medication, they need to urge them to see a physician as soon as physically possible and alert an RA, administrator, or dean. The longing to start a new life at college as an unmedicated person is understandable, but the risks are high. Most students who do so go off the rails very early on in the first semester. It can be tough to recover all that they lose in the process in terms of course-work, friendships, the trust of the people around them, and a feeling of solid ground under their feet. Some even have to withdraw from the semester and start college again later on, depending on the college's rules for readmission.

A Word or Two About Sex

It goes without saying that the attitudes toward sex among students will be as varied as they are toward alcohol and other drugs. I put them in the same category because college is that stereotypical time of testing boundaries. Most students experiment with sex, alcohol, and other drugs during their years on campus because they have the freedom to do so, and the opportunity presents itself relatively fre-quently. These activities also have in common the fact that they all are risky—physically, emotionally, socially, and academically. Every-one should take the time to define for themselves how much risk they want to take in these years.

Some students graduate without having had any significant sexual experiences, and others hook up with three or four different people a week for a semester or two running. I have talked extensively with students who regretted some or many of their sexual experiences and others who did not feel the slightest bit of remorse when think-ing back on their partners and activities. College officials do not and should not stand in judgment of any of them. Students stand in judg-ment of themselves, and that is the point. They will be harsh on themselves, so forethought is an essential practice, but one that eludes many eighteen- to twenty-two-year-olds.

Whatever attitudes they encounter during the college years, the important thing is for them to articulate their own approaches and preferences toward sex and observe the ways they change. They may evolve a great deal or not at all. Whatever the case, they will hopefully be true to themselves. It may sound trite, but that is the first and most important principle. Sexual intelligence is about foresight and forethought. These are private, personal choices that they will ideally make with a clear head and true heart.

The national estimates are all over the place, and who knows how accurate any of them are. But I would venture to guess that there is a lot less sex happening on college campuses than people imagine. Most of the statistics suggest that as well. A far bigger problem is loneliness and not feeling connected. But for students who are or intend to be sexually active, health services offices offer lots of support, information, and care. Peer health advocates are a great resource for the student who has questions or concerns.

College sex is in the news every day, especially with respect to the measures colleges are undertaking to raise awareness of and prevent sexual assaults. We have all heard the statistics. One in four women and one in six men will be sexually assaulted in their lifetimes. One-half of sexual assaults involve alcohol use by the victim and perpetrator. Eighty percent of victims know their assailants. These startling and disturbing numbers have led almost every college in the United States to create mandatory educational programs for students, administrators, and faculty alike. The initiatives might not be perfect, but they are important. If your child is particularly moved by this national issue, they can probably find a way to get involved in educational outreach and prevention efforts. Even if they do not want to spend free time on this, they will hopefully do their best to instill in peers the importance of paying attention to whatever programs the college offers. They might save themselves or a friend from a lifetime of horrible memories.

Why and How to Curb Compulsive Sociability

Every generation introduces innovative forms of communication and expression. As each one comes on the scene, there are inevitably people who bemoan the loss of a grand past and predict that nothing good will come of it, while others excitedly espouse the virtues of the new. Even when the printing press came on the publishing scene in the early fifteenth century, it was predicted that humans would suffer irreparable psychological and physical damage from information overload. And when the telephone was invented, people feared it would threaten our society as we knew it, infringe on our privacy (which some still feel it does), and promote crime that would destroy the fabric of our civilization. Naysayers and optimists have expounded on the inevitable detrimental effects and the yet unknown benefits of everything from the telegraph to the television to the cellphone.

No one can deny that options for communicating our thoughts, feelings, and images abound. By the time this book is published, there will be more. We are living in an age, and perhaps have always lived in an age, of what William Deresiewicz, a frequent college speaker and author of *Excellent Sheep: The Miseducation of the American Elite and the Way to a Meaningful Life,* calls "compulsive sociability." He is referring to the ubiquitous and unrelenting electronic communication practiced by many college students. I don't think that constant contact with peers is anything new, but I fully agree with Deresiewicz's emphasis on having what I call a "practice of solitude."

What does this have to do with your child and college? It's really quite simple. Anytime we find ourselves in a new home, town, or organization, we have a lot to learn, people to meet, and things to do. We are surrounded by so much that is different that being able to stay in touch with ourselves and make the right decisions for us and our family means we turn to conscious or unconscious practices of introspection and reflection. The same is true for college students. They are on the go all the time—and have been that way for years. But now they really need to stay in touch with themselves.

This does not mean that they have to trek to the top of the Himalayas to ponder the big questions in life. What it can mean is that they find ten minutes a day to be alone. They silence their phone, shut down the computer, and think about the day, a conversation they had with someone, the work before them, the number of weeks until they go home, their high school friends, their new acquaintances, where they might want to intern this summer, or how they feel about what they have done and learned so far. In short, reflecting on something meaningful to them every day for at least a few minutes can make all the difference. It doesn't matter whether they write in a journal or sit in a temple or chapel or walk or run or row or skate.

Any practice of this sort will help them stay in touch with their feelings and thoughts and strengthen their connection to themselves, which will help fortify them for the inevitable challenges that college presents. The point is to continually check the alignment of their expectations, values, and goals against their actions and pursuits. Are their activities, in the classroom and out, in accord with their true self? Everyone has an authentic self. College is a place for the focused discovery and realization of that self. From that will flow the right decisions about their future personal and professional life.

A practice of solitude will also help them develop their resourcefulness and resilience. When expectations, activities, and values are aligned, they will be able to achieve high levels of success in the all-important first year and naturally continue to access these throughout the pursuit of the degree. It is simply a matter of being aware and conscious of oneself and one's actions, beliefs, and heart, as well as the way they intersect and interact with the world around us. Whether you call it solitude, mindfulness, reflection, or introspection is not important. What is essential is for college students to find their way to themselves every day.

I know what you're thinking: *If I suggest to my son or daughter that they develop a practice of mindfulness and solitude for a few moments a day, they will think I'm crazy.* Perhaps so, but every time I have successfully convinced a college student to do this, they have reported back to me surprising and immediate benefits.

Food for Thought

- Does your son or daughter have a current practice of solitude?
- If not, in what way do they think they could?
- If they already have a practice, is it proving to be doable in college?
- Do they want to try new ones?
- Are there options for a practice of solitude available on the new campus? A park? Interesting cityscapes? A single room? A chapel, church, synagogue, or temple?
- Are those options accessible every day?
- Where else can your student imagine going to have a bit of time to themselves?

I encourage all students to develop a practice of solitude they can depend on so they don't miss a single day of centering themselves.

Finding Their Niche on the Global Stage

As new college students delve ever-more deeply into their first-year courses, many begin to grapple with the question of how they might get involved in some of the thorny issues of their era. This freshman tendency has only increased over the past decade as campus activism continues to thrust major and tough national and international problems into the forefront of our consciousness.

The complexities of our globalizing world present college students with infinite possibilities and a lot of freedom. That means both exciting vistas and tough choices. Because countries, peoples, and their activities are increasingly intertwined, your child's education and careers may span cultures and continents. While selecting an academic focus will be essential, students confront big questions before those decisions can be reached. While they are learning about the history of human thought and grappling with philosophical, environmental, scientific, ethical, moral, and other important questions in college courses and in conversations with peers, it will become even clearer to them now than it was in high school that they have to decide for themselves what their roles in the world should be and what they need to prepare themselves to play them.

The more learned they become, the more aware they are of world issues that go well beyond their own family, town, or college. They will learn about things that affect the whole globe. Justice and injustice, humanity and inhumanity, equality and inequities, climate change, wealth and poverty, satiation and hunger, consumption and supply of resources, animal welfare, cultures, languages, war, love, peace, and so forth. Questions about many of these weighty matters will present themselves in some form or another during the years on campus in coursework, extracurriculars, and personal conversations. As a result, each student inevitably wrestles with their perspective on these issues and whether or not such topics interest them. If they do, the next question that comes to mind is what roles they hope to play in the complex interplay of these issues in their adult lives. As Harold Shapiro, a former university president, wrote so eloquently: "Today as never before we are bound together in a vastly enlarged moral community composed of groups with a wide variety of traditions and different views regarding substantive moral issues." In a sense, one of the most important missions of college is to enhance a student's understanding of the ways we are all connected and to help students find their niche within it.

Let's take the random example of malaria. Say a student learns in an African Civilizations class that the deaths of over a half million children from this infectious disease could be prevented every year through the simple use of mosquito nets. This particular subject

grabs their attention, so they wonder how they might make a difference in the lives of the suffering due to the lack of something that
costs little to make and is available widely in the developed world.
Here are some possibilities they may entertain—for their college
years and beyond:

- Hold a fundraiser on campus or in the local community to raise
  awareness and money.
- Post information about the cause on social media sites.
- Join or start a student organization devoted to helping.
- Create educational programs that nongovernmental organiza-
  tions can deliver in-country.
- Work with an aid group in the summer to distribute the nets
  and run programs on their proper use.
- Write grant proposals for a nonprofit that supports this cause.
- Design cheaper, better nets as part of a project for an engineer-
  ing, architecture, or design class.
- Convince a future employer to match employee donations to it.
- Get involved down the road with a corporation's philanthropic
  office, and get them interested in it.
- Go into finance, make a lot of money, and donate substantial
  amounts to the cause.

In other words, they can choose to participate on the advocacy
side and/or on the funding side. Sylvia is an example of a student
who ended up very much on the advocacy side of things. She had
gone to college intent on becoming a doctor. When she didn't fare
well in her first chemistry course and then did horribly in the second, she began to question whether medicine was the best direction
for her. In the meantime, she had been placed into a freshman seminar on the inequities in education across the United States. Over
dinner one night in the dining hall, she was approached by another
student who wanted to recruit her to work with Teach for America
(TFA), an organization devoted to educational access and equity.

Sylvia got so excited by what she heard that she signed up for an info session the following week. She then applied for and was thrilled to get a summer internship at a TFA administrative office in Mississippi. When she graduated from college, she spent two years teaching in an impoverished area and then became a staff member of the TFA administration. Eventually she went to graduate school to earn a doctorate in education.

If you had told Sylvia in her senior year of high school that she was not going to be a doctor but rather would become a lifelong educator in pursuit of leveling the educational playing field in the United States, she would have thought you were crazy. These sorts of shifts in interest and passion are not unusual; in fact, they are quite common! Let's take another example.

Edward went to college with the long-held idea that he would get his undergraduate and graduate degrees in the United States and then return to his home country to pursue a career in politics. He felt he could do the most good for his community if he worked in government, where he could influence the making of policy and legislation. As he got to know juniors and seniors through some of his courses and activities, he kept hearing them talk about "i-banking"— some were preparing for i-banking interviews, while others had already gotten a summer internship at an i-bank. He didn't have a clue what they were talking about. When he learned that they were all planning to enter investment banking, he was shocked and began to ask why. Could they all simply be so materialistic and superficial? Of course, they all talked about the financial rewards of that career path, but many mentioned something more interesting. They felt that they could do the most good in the world if they earned big money to later disburse in ways that could improve society through donations and advocacy—in addition to being able to provide for their families and communities. As Edward discovered through his coursework, he was particularly talented in and fascinated by economics, so he eventually chose that as his major. Upon graduation, he secured a position at an investment bank. Now in his late twenties, he is earning enough money so that he is already able to make a difference—not only for his family but also for his community and other causes he supports, such as gender-based-violence and global-poverty awareness, topics that had moved him in other college courses.

What Edward decided in the end, perhaps consciously but maybe not, was to live according to a concept of "effective altruism," a philosophical and social movement that emphasizes using reason and an understanding of one's values to make the biggest possible positive impact on things in the world that are important to us. Edward made the personal decision to pursue a career that offered high compensation not only because he was talented in that area and enjoyed it but also because it would do the most good down the line. Sylvia, on the other hand, decided she wanted to work as an agent of change from within, so devoted her professional life to education and policymaking that would effect change in areas she loved.

Both Sylvia and Edward are great examples of people who successfully negotiated the kinds of issues many college students are surprised to find themselves grappling with. It makes sense if you think about it. Once they have been exposed to global issues, they naturally ask themselves how they might fit into the equation. Given their new knowledge of the world's issues and, especially, the pain and suffering of others, they often start with considering whether they want to engage in local or global communities. Should they become an advocate, a donor, or both? For which causes?

Student activism is currently experiencing a sharp increase across the country, so every new student will inevitably become aware at the very least of the salient topics on their campuses, which might be free speech, gun rights, global poverty, animal cruelty, racial inequality, or gender-based violence, just to name a few. Whether they get involved on campus or not, it is also likely that their exposure to the global issues of our time will pique their interest, and that knowledge will unavoidably be carried forward into their professional lives.

Their career can be the means to make positive change in the world, on a local, national, or global platform, whether they end up focusing exclusively on their family and/or eventually serve as a promoter from within (like Sylvia) or from the outside (like Edward). The outcome will depend on what interests are awakened, reinforced, and deepened in the coming years.

The hallmark of a good college experience is precisely this—to stimulate and cultivate passions and to help students figure out what to do about them. Everyone has them, things that move us to live and act in particular ways. As Derrick Bell wrote in *Ethical Ambition: Living a Life of Meaning and Worth*, "Passion is not an event, but an energy; and it's an energy that exists in all of us, all the time. The question is not whether we have it but whether we access it, and how we channel it." I believe fervently in Bell's statement appearing a little further along in that same book, when he says, "The sacrifice of passion is a kind of psychic suicide." He goes on: "The playing field is not level, but no one—even those in whose favor the field tilts—can control how much passion we bring to the game, and how much pleasure we take from it."

College will expose your child to millions of ideas, some of which will resonate and help them decide how they will spend their time and energy in the future. As they have proceeded through this semester, you may have heard about some of those moments. They may have given you pause as you noticed how your child's interests were changing and expanding. To be successfully open to such moments, young people need to admit that they are—without a doubt, and somewhat terrifyingly—living with a degree of ambiguity and uncertainty. This is much easier said than done. But they can rest assured that they will eventually figure it out. Your child has infinite possibilities in terms of their future and can decide to define themselves as a change-maker from within and/or a donor to causes that hold meaning for them. Watching them grow and change and wrestle with the possibilities can be exciting and gratifying.

Thanksgiving Notes

- If your child comes home for this four-day break, you may already notice differences in their focus and thinking. You may want to see what emerges in conversation with respect to social activism, drugs, alcohol, sex, relationships, and other issues.

- Don't be surprised if you sense some tension coming from them. They are growing and changing quickly, and it's not always comfortable. You may want to gently inquire about things, but you may just want to see what emerges naturally.

- Expect that they might have a lot of schoolwork to do. Thanksgiving falls between midterms and finals, so they may have studying, reading, or writing to finish before going back.

- Of course, you will let them sleep as much as they want, but they may also be excited about partying with their high school friends. The Friday night after Thanksgiving is that infamous and quintessential moment to enjoy old friends and reminisce. It's a much-needed moment of connecting with familiar signposts of the past. For many, it's the last time they will see that particular group of buddies, but for now it's a comforting experience that reminds them of where they came from and also, mostly unconsciously, shows them how far they have come since high school graduation.

- If your child can't come home for Thanksgiving, try not to worry. Most colleges have lovely programs for the many students who aren't able to leave campus. And many roommates and friends will extend invitations.

Back to You

At the same time that your child is wrestling with the right role for them locally and globally, you can now spend a few moments focusing on your engagement in your various communities. Having invested some time in enhancing aspects of your health and professional well-being, you will now hopefully have the energy and focus to breathe new life into building your social world.

Social engagement is a form of play that you can spend an hour on here and there, so it doesn't have to start as a time-consuming commitment. As already mentioned, establishing new habits of mind and action takes months, but it can start in a concrete way right now. It may seem silly to spend time on a notion of play for adults, but as many psychologists have pointed out, it is absolutely essential for the emotional, physical, and spiritual well-being of adults and children alike. It offers us time to rejuvenate our minds, our spirits, and our bodies. Stuart Brown put it succinctly when he wrote: "[Play] is intensely pleasurable. It energizes us and enlivens us. It eases our burdens. It renews our natural sense of optimism and opens us up to new possibilities. . . . But that is just the beginning of the story. Neuroscientists, developmental biologists, psychologists, social scientists, and researchers from every point of the scientific compass now know that play is a profound biological process. . . . It shapes the brain and makes animals smarter and more adaptable. . . . [I]t fosters empathy and makes possible complex social groups. For us, play lies at the core of creativity and innovation."

When you think back on the times in your life when you had the most fun, where were you—as a child, a teenager, and a young adult? I can recall sledding, ice-skating, and fort-building in feet of snow when I was under ten years of age, running into the house to tear off the snowsuit so that my mother could throw it into the dryer and warm it up for me, and downing a cup of hot chocolate to fortify myself for the next round. As a teenager, I played games with friends in the summer—from chess to bowling to tree-climbing and making a clubhouse by painting the sewer pipe at the culvert at the end of the block. In college, the play was centered on music, dancing, and bike-riding with friends. All of these memories have a carefree and fun feeling about them. I feel energized just thinking about them. Those are the instances of pure play that are inextricably linked to my sense of connection to myself and others. What are yours? Where did they take place? How old were you? Are any of those people or activities still in your life?

As adults, most of us are not as good at playing as we were as children. In the United States, we take adulthood very seriously. Time to work, work, work, raise kids, attend to our civic duties, bear down on our self-improvement efforts, and work some more. What would benefit us all is to intentionally dedicate some moments each week to playing.

Speaking of Play . . .

- When you think back on your playful moments as a child, teenager, and young adult, what were the most significant ones? What were you doing, and who were you playing with?
- How would you describe the sense of play in those instances?
- Have there been similar experiences as an adult? If so, what were you doing, and with whom?
- What does or would offer you that feeling of pure play now?

Even an hour a week of playing will mean you have made strides in the right direction. And they don't have to cost a lot. A few suggestions to get your thought process started: Take a bike ride in a new area, do a walking tour of unfamiliar neighborhoods, sign up for a watercolor or oil-painting course, institute a weekly card game, take a cooking lesson, join a dance class, reignite a friendship with a fun person, do some jigsaw puzzles with the family, try pole dancing, or bounce on a trampoline. Any activity that helps you connect with others in a carefree, unselfconscious way will do. Here are some examples:

- Sue spent more time biking and walking with college friends and relatives.
- Huey discovered a love of hosting theme parties.
- Charlotte deepened her relationships with people she had only just met.
- Claudia found herself going out to eat more spontaneously with friends.
- Karl delved into his family tree and reached out to some new-found relatives.

As you try this out, you will see that you reap the benefits immediately. As your child explores their new world, you can reexplore and re-create yours. The time you invest in play will not only distract you temporarily and healthily from the transition your family is undergoing but also help you discover new aspects of yourself and make you laugh. What could be better than that?

Some Final Thoughts on Play

- Adults often let the practice of playing fall by the wayside, but play is important not only to children but to all of us.
- Play releases creative juices and enhances our spiritual, mental, and physical health.
- You will have the opportunity to discover or rediscover parts of yourself by dedicating time to play at this time of your life.

CHAPTER 8

Finishing Strong

The end of the first semester is staring you down. Your child is coming home soon, so you look forward to preparing for their arrival and organizing activities, visits, parties, and meals. But before you do that, it is time to help your child finish the semester strong. Then, with a hearty pat or two on the back, you can start putting pieces of your new life in place and celebrate. This does not mean that you won't prepare for your child's arrival. I mean, a little dusting never hurt anything. But reveling in your own success will only make the homecoming sweeter as you celebrate theirs as well.

The Initial College Grades

By December, students are so close to going home that they can taste it. They are desperate for some well-deserved rest, good food, and general merriment. But between now and then, a single-minded approach is the best so that they can finish strong. You have been practicing letting go for months now, but this is as good an excuse as any to reengage your helicopter skills. Most students really need that right now, because in spite of the fact that they are spent, physically, emotionally, and intellectually, they must focus. They have a lot of work to do before the end.

It's time to encourage your child to turn their attention in a single-minded way to the academic work before them. They should exclude everything other than schoolwork. And I mean everything. Between this moment and the hour they leave for winter break, they should only think about the remaining academic requirements. If they can forget about the draining complexities of friendships, love, family, and anything else that is pulling at them, they will be able to dedicate all of their energy to being a student. People who might need and deserve some attention will just have to understand and wait.

What You Can Do to Help

Encourage your child to:

1. List all of the remaining work and deadlines.
2. Create a schedule that includes sleep, class time, and meals.
3. Include a visit to each of their professor's office hours at least once in the remaining days to talk about ways to focus their time on the most important things for the final exam or to discuss a paper topic.
4. Fill the remaining hours with writing papers, studying for exams, and completing any other assignments before bidding goodbye to the semester.

If there are any deadlines they do not think they will be able to meet, advise them to talk with their advisor or professor *immediately*. Depending on the policies at the college, this may mean reaching out to a dean, a professor, or both. Be sure they look up how to request extensions; the instructions should be clearly delineated somewhere on the website. They should also pay attention to the implications of an Incomplete on their transcript.

They should kindly let their family, friends, and significant others know that they are entering a time of focused attention on work, and can't wait to spend more time with them over the break or in the coming semester.

Being single-minded in their approach to the end of the semester will mean that they will feel good about themselves, knowing they did the best they could with the time they had left. Also, grades will inevitably reflect how much time they put in. There is a third benefit: Knowing what it took to finish strong may encourage students to start this process earlier next semester and, one would hope, without your help and advice. In other words, help them do this well, once— because there is no doubt that the productive energy they expend is directly proportional to their personal satisfaction, the amount they learn, and the grades they earn.

And while we're on the subject of grades, let's prepare you for the possibility that your child's final marks might not be what they had hoped. Because once your child's grades come in, if they are one of the many who are less than thrilled by the results of their work, there is recourse. Since you know that grade grubbing is undignified, you can approach grading issues with knowledge about the relevant policies and procedures and with no small dab of humility and respect. Believe it or not, the best ways to respond to requests for higher scores than earned is a common topic of conversation among college instructors.

Here are the steps your child can take to address grade concerns:

1. Find the grading rubric or guidelines in the syllabus or course management system for the course they are concerned about.

While it is a student's responsibility to meet the demands of the course, it is the professor's job to ensure that students know how they are being evaluated and then to assess them accordingly. Print out the grading information.

2. Get all the work together from the relevant course—anything that was evaluated and earned a grade, a check mark, comments, and so on. List all of those results on the grading information page.

3. If participation in class was a factor, they should think back on how many times they missed class, how much they contributed to the discussions, and how many times they met with the TA or professor during office hours. Does the grader know their name and have some sense of how invested in the course they were? With that information in mind, have them give themselves a fair grade for that aspect of the course.

4. Now have them take a good look at all the work and read any feedback the grader offered.

5. Do the calculation on the grading info sheet.

Is the result the same as the professor's? If so, then they are done, and it's time to talk about ways to do better next semester. Which areas were the weakest? The strongest? Is this course in an intended or actual major or minor? If so, it will be especially crucial for them to figure out how to improve if the grade they earned makes them less than proud. A follow-up conversation with the instructor is always a great first place to start after reflecting on their overall accomplishments in the course. If they meet with the professor soon enough after the end of the semester, they will likely get some useful feedback. Memories fade, especially given how busy faculty are, so students should get in there quickly after break.

Is the result higher than the one in the student information system? If so, it is time for *the student* (not you!) to reach out to the grader(s) by crafting a kind and solicitous email, avoiding anything that even vaguely resembles grade grubbing, which would not have the intended effect. I repeat: you must not write to or call the professor yourself, even if you are sorely tempted to do so. It's your child's responsibility to inquire in the gentlest possible terms whether they might meet with the professor to talk about the outcome of the course. (Note that most colleges have deadlines for grading inquiries.)

Every college approaches grade disputes differently. In most cases, the term "grade dispute" is pretty strong. In any case, if they look up "grade disputes" or "grade appeals" on the college's website, they will usually find a step-by-step process. Normally, the grade dispute or appeals process has multiple steps, but it should always start with a conversation between the student and the grader. I know this is difficult to do. After all, the student is in an evaluative relationship with the professor and the TA. Most universities and colleges will require that they have that conversation first, however, so you will want to have all your ducks in a row—the work, grades, feedback, rubric, and calculations. It is easiest to start this conversation if they already have a good relationship with the faculty member, which is one of the many reasons I always advise students to visit faculty during office hours at least two or three times in the semester.

What if they do not hear back from the TA or professor within a week? Colleges pretty much shut down for winter break, so do not be alarmed if the email doesn't generate an immediate response. If a deadline for grading inquiries is looming, reach out to a dean or another administrator who is more likely to be online during the holiday period.

After that initial one-on-one conversation, if the student hasn't gotten the outcome they believe they deserve, the next step might be the advising staff, the provost's office, the dean of the college, a department chair, a director of undergraduate studies, a dean of the faculty, et cetera, et cetera, et cetera. Every college is different. That's another reason it's important to find the grade appeals info before embarking on the process.

I've left the most important part of this process to the end—the educational benefit of a grade calculation. Through the in-depth consideration of their work in the course, your child hopefully has learned something that they can bring into future coursework. Even if the grade dispute process leaves them with the same grade, it will have been worth the trouble if they've taken away something beneficial for the future.

Next semester, encourage them to find and print out the grading rubrics for all courses before the first class meeting and keep them available throughout so that they can determine how much time and energy to put into the different aspects of the class. Plus, going to see each instructor at least two or three times a term to talk over the course will help a lot. If any of the grading seems unclear along the way, they can talk about it during those office hours as well.

This raises another question: Are college grades important? The true answer is maybe, maybe not. While students are pursuing a degree, colleges will put them on probation if their GPA falls below a certain number (2.0 is typical). If bad performance continues, suspension or dismissal is a possibility. Most schools pay less attention to the first-semester grades and won't put a student on academic probation for less-than-stellar outcomes. They know that the first semester is an adjustment, so they'll give the student a pass. After that, the academic-standing guidelines will be applied in earnest.

When a student is planning for the first "real job" out of college, they should know that first employers and graduate schools usually require the applicant's GPA. They likely use it to weed out applicants, as a shortcut to reduce the number of full applications they have to consider seriously. After that, the GPA rarely plays a role. (If you got a degree, think back: When was the last time you had to share yours? Do you even remember it? I don't remember mine!) Obviously, no one goes to college to do poorly or to just skate by. The real goal is for your child to do as well as they can so that they can feel proud of their accomplishments upon graduation and beyond.

Turning to Your Family and Love Relationships

There is no better month to focus on the family and the loves in your life than December. Whether you are religious, agnostic, or atheist, this is the quintessential American time to get together with friends and family to eat, drink, and be merry. Now that you have renewed your commitment to your health, spent some energy on your career and financial well-being, and enhanced your community and social engagement, it is time to celebrate. But with whom? And how?

If you have begun to establish new relationships in the enhancement of your world, now's the time to make or confirm plans to get together at end-of-year gatherings and celebrations. See if it is feasible to accept invitations to December holiday parties that come in from your worlds of work and play. It is okay to schedule some events, coffee dates, cocktails, or dinners for days when your new college student will be home.

Returning to the work you did in summer, are there relatives you want to invite over, make a lunch date with, or simply send a card to say you are thinking of them? Have you ironed out long-standing familial conflicts to the extent that you can include people you might not have invited last year? Did you connect with people in your family tree? Are there cousins, aunts, uncles who have nowhere to go to celebrate the holidays?

Taking steps to solidify the place of newcomers in your life will send a strong signal, first of all to the recipients of your invitations. They will be flattered by the attention and pleased to know of your interest. It will also be a robust sign to yourself that there is joy to be had in the establishment of an independent life. Finally, it will serve the highly beneficial purpose of indicating something very important to your child. You will be communicating that it is healthy and positive to invite additional people into your life and that some of those relationships will not involve your children. This enables freshmen to understand that it is okay for them to share news of their burgeoning friendships and love interests with you. New college students sometimes feel uncomfortable about having developed a network of friendships and support without the knowledge or involvement of the parent. They may even report that guilt caused them to restrain themselves when describing the joy they were finding in their now more autonomous lives. The mutual acknowledgment of important connections with other people exclusive of each other is the ultimate sign of healthy attachment and detachment. This is not to say that you will not be intertwined with each other. Not at all. It signifies that your relationship has advanced to a more mature developmental juncture, one in which the recognition of distinct and separate adult lives prevails. Your bond can be strengthened by sharing the news of the new people in your respective lives.

Detaching does not mean that you don't care for each other. It signifies that you love each other as adults. You will always be their parent, but this shift in the relationship will enable other things to fall into place—in particular, the continuation of a secure attachment where your child sees you as a base to which they can always return. They will begin to grasp that they can go out into the world as many times as they desire, and you will be there when they get back, and you will relish the stories of the adventures they had while away. In other words, detaching in this way does not mean there is a lack of healthy attachment. On the contrary, it ensures that a healthy bond will continue into the future.

Solidifying the love relationship in your life or introducing a new one has an additional benefit. The way you conduct yourself in matters of love serves as a significant model for your child that they will take into their love lives as well. If you have done things that you are less than proud of, this might be a good time for you to address those with your child. Open conversation will send important messages to your teenager that mistakes, humility, and forgiveness are part of life, and it may relieve any existing tension about choices you may have made. It takes a long time for humans to learn to love well. How many people actually master it in the first three or four decades of life? Reflecting on the quality of your loves thus far and the way others, especially your child, must perceive you may be painful, but like all grueling processes, the benefits outweigh the difficulties.

As you prepare for your child to come home, you can also be fairly sure that interpersonal relationship drama on campus has likely consumed a lot of time and energy. Your child will need you to be open to talking about it. They may even have been in some uncomfortable sexual situations and be confused about the nature of their feelings toward someone they have met in the past few months. Sharing your thoughts on love and relationships will model the openness you hope your child will have in conversation with you so that you can help them work things out for the return to campus.

Home Again

Even though every parent and every child is obviously different, there are a number of truisms that apply to the first between-semesters break. The following are designed so that you and your child align your expectations of the time you will be living under the same roof again for more than a couple of days.

1. There will be some anxiety, stress, and/or tension as both parties recognize that things may have changed. The child may be weirded out that some part of the home has been altered (even their room, though that is less and less common these days). The parent may be startled to see physical, emotional, and intellectual differences. Try not to judge them, at least out loud. Keep them to yourself unless they bring them up or you are worried about their well-being.

2. The freshman will have to rest and sleep. A lot. Many parents call their physicians when their child doesn't get up much in the first two or three or even four days. Sleeping is normal in most cases. The energy they have expended in the previous four

months is beyond enormous. They are spent and need some extended downtime. Be sure to allow for that in the schedule.

3. If you've argued and not resolved issues since September, there may be some awkwardness. Take heart that you will now have time to put to bed any lingering conflicts once your child has rested.

4. They may want to spend a lot of time virtually or in real life with new college friends. Be clear with them before they come home about the time you have available to them and ask them to reserve time for any plans you have made or ideas you have.

5. After four months of dining hall food, it is likely that they will want some comfort food. But take note: Ask if their dietary habits have changed and what they would like to see in the pantry when they get home. College students commonly experiment with new food regimens, with paleo, vegan, and pescatarian options being particularly popular these days. You don't want to stock the fridge with meat only to learn that your child has forsworn it, at least for the time being.

6. Their dirty laundry will be plentiful, unless your child is truly unusual. You may want to consider whether you are going to do it for them, have someone else do it, or have them do it themselves. Communicate that ahead of time.

7. If your college freshman has devoted himself to school as you hoped he would, he probably hasn't had a moment to think about holiday gifts. If your family exchanges presents, you may want to figure out with him how to remedy this so that he feels included and can participate.

The biggest obstacle to a peaceful holiday season is the misalignment of expectations between parents and their college children. Above all, keep in mind that you may want to spend more or less time with them than they plan. This can be a source of friction and deeply hurt feelings on both sides. It is best to broach this topic with them well before finals, at least so that they can keep it in mind as they travel homeward.

Once the college student has rested, enjoyed some comfort food, and come to life a little, your family can hopefully enjoy one another's company and revel in stories of your student's fall semester. They have begun to establish new acquaintances and even friendships, delved into topics they may never have discovered before, and begun to think of themselves in slightly or dramatically different terms. It will be fascinating to hear how their plans for their future may have changed.

By the same token, your child will hopefully be excited to hear of all the things you have undertaken since they moved onto campus. When you share your inroads into your health, professional, financial, social, and community well-being, they may be a mixture of happy, relieved, and even a bit jealous. Ultimately, you can rest assured that you are giving them permission to be independent, loving adults who can go away and come back knowing that you will still be there for them as long as you can.

ACKNOWLEDGMENTS

Every book owes its existence to many people. This one came into being because thousands of college students and their parents shared their struggles and successes with me. I am honored to have been a part of their journeys.

There are a few whose names I must mention because they have meant so very much to me: Danielle Hamilton and her mom, Sharmain; Emery Whalen and her mom, Emery Clarke; Thomas Spry and his mom, Penny; John Wachter and his dad, John; Will and Jamie Mazur and their dad, Marc; Elizabeth Rossiter and her mom, Kay; Charif Shanahan and his mom and dad, Naima and Steven; Benjamin Gittelson and his mom, Clare Rubin; the Jennings, Byron Austin, Maxwell Banaszak, Aaron Bianco, Colton Bishop, Richelle Campbell (née Blanchard), Eric Chase, Robbie Collins, Dennis Dacarett-Galeano, Kyle Detwiler, Bayard Dodge, Anna Fraser, Alex Frouman, Meagan Rose Gamache, Ben Gittelson, Adam Goldenberg, Dafna Gottesman, Whitney Green, Greg Gudis, Karishma Habbu, Linnea Hartmark, Oliver Jennings, Jeremy Johnson, John Jovanovic, Elsbeth Kane, Brandon Lafving, Carla LaRoche, Sharon Liao, Rachel Lyon, Erica McGibbon, Annalisa Castillo Meier, Kyle Morgan, Nikki Mueller, Evan Munro, Alexis Okeowo, Dominic Perkovic, Andrew Perlmutter, Karleta Peterson, Tyler Pewarski, Rabah Qadir, Roberto Rosas, Ash Sarohia, Miriam Schive, Christopher Schroer, Smita Sen, Amanda Suarez, Leizhi Sun, Richard Sun, Katie Beck Sutler, Lauren Taney, Ian Tyler, Sarah van der Ploeg, Tom

Vogl, Sarah Weiss, Monique Wilson, Sue Yang, Kenneth Zauderer, Noah Zgrablich, and Chris Zombik. I have learned so much from each of you about how colleges and universities can help students succeed.

I've been fortunate to have had countless thoughtful colleagues and friends at every turn: at Binghamton, Paul Jordan, Barbara Kaufman, Joan Kaufman, Debbie Loss-Rimler, Randall Moore, and Paul Sweeny; at CUNY-Hunter, Peter and Katie Basquin, Ernst Fedor Hoffmann, Dorothy James, Eckhard Kuhn-Osius, Annette Kym, and Michael Skafidas; at Princeton, Yvan Bamps, Talia Bloch, Robin Boudette, Maggie Browning, Ron Connor, Bob Criso, Michael Curschmann, Janet Dickerson, Sean Dilley, Michael Doran, Alec Dun, Claire Fowler, Rebecca Graves-Bayazitoğlu, Jeff Guynn, Lars Hedin, Lisa Herschbach, Karen Humphreys, Sanjeev Kulkarni, Joshua Landis, Tom Levin, Chiara Levy, John and Jan Logan, John Lyon, Nancy Malkiel, Michael McNeill, Eyda Merediz, Joe Michels, Sara Ogger, Frank Ordiway, Darryl Peterkin, Paul Brandeis Raushenbush, Jason Read, Susan Scherer, Maggie Schleissner, Joerg and Latha Schmitz, Danielle Walker, Martin Weigert, and Bob Wickenden; at Harvard, David Ager, Inge-Lise Ameer, Peter Aranow, Steven Bloomfield, Tony Broh, Brian Casey, Sally Donahue, Bob Doyle, Bill Fitzsimmons, Anna Fraser, Jay Harris, Georgene Herschbach, R. J. Jenkins, Stephanie Kenen, Marlyn Lewis, Maya Mangawang, Caitlin McDonough, Joshua McIntosh, Paul McLoughlin, Bob Mitchell, Suzy Nelson, Patricia O'Brien, Faith Oliver, Donald Pfister, David Pilbeam, Margaret Vendryes, and Judy Wolfe; at Columbia, Daniel Barkowitz, Jeff Boland, Allan Cassorla, Darleny Cepin, Jessica De Palo, Michael Dunn, Richard Eichler, Robert Ferraiuolo, Suzanne Goldberg, Paula Goodman, Jeri Henry, Barry Kane, Greg Lamb, Laila Maher, Pete Mangurian, Terry Martinez, Hazel May, Peter Michaelides, Radhika Patel, Victoria Rosner, Laurie Schaffler, Anna Schmidt-MacKenzie, Jeffrey Scott, Dan White, and Stephen Yablon; and at the New School, Nikki Cherry, Keisha Davenport-Ramirez, Mike Fakih, Rachel Francois, Rebecca Hunter, Ruthie Kroah, Florence Leclerc-Dickler, Ilana Levitt, Marisa LoBianco, Jennifer MacDonald, Angelica Peña, Michelle Relyea, Donald Resnick, Maureen Sheridan, Leah Weich, and Thelma Woods. I so appreciate the time we had.

To the colleagues and friends at my new professional home, NPAP: Robin Berg, Saša Bogdanović, Jonathan Clarke, Jeffrey DeRoche, Adi Flesher, Gina Gold, Glenda Hydler, Susan Kassouf, Ursula Katayama-O'Connor, Kat Lau, Olivier Letang, Tom Lutri, Douglas Maxwell, Sue Mitchell, Matt Paldy, Sherman Pheiffer, Daniel Polyak, Dennis Raptis, Gavriel Reisner, Kimber Riddle, Jan Roth, Jared Russell, Aderyn Wood, Traci Yoder, Shari Zimmerman, thank you all for welcoming me into the fold.

To my very special dog friends, Karen Barkey, Kevin Dornan, L. J. Ganser, Ian Jackman, Tony Marx, John Mathews, Mary Peppito, Sarah Phillips, Albert Tsuei, Kara Welsh—our beloved canines brought us together in such wonderful ways.

To Jane Dystel of Dystel, Goderich, and Bourret, the most wonderful literary agent I could have hoped for, and Marnie Cochran, a dream of an editor—I can't thank you enough for believing in this book.

To Kerry Walk, the first and ever-clear-sighted champion of this project; and to those who have traveled countless miles with me—Joan Davidson, Jackie Gotthold, Katie and Kristina Naplatarski, Tim Reiland, and the whole Avitsur family—Monica, Haim, and their wonderful children, Ezra and Avner, what can I say? I simply can't express how grateful I am. You inspire me.

And, finally, to my family, the Abbitts, McGahees, Rineres, and Stepnowskis, and to my husband, Benedict, who valiantly put up with the inevitable vicissitudes of bringing a book from concept to print—thank you!

ADDITIONAL RESOURCES

General Information

Here are some of the most used and helpful websites for general college information and data:

College Confidential, CollegeConfidential.com

CollegeData, CollegeData.com

College Parents of America, collegeparents.org

College Parent Central, collegeparentcentral.com

The federal government's College Navigator, nces.ed.gov/college navigator

The Institute for College Access and Success has great resources, including College Insight, college-insight.org

Great Reads on College

Andrew Delbanco's book *College: What It Was, Is, and Should Be* (Princeton University Press, 2012) is an incredibly thoughtful and brisk consideration of the past, current, and ideal future goals of college in America.

Frank Bruni's *Where You Go Is Not Who You'll Be: An Antidote to the College Admissions Mania* (Grand Central Publishing, 2016) is a must for anyone who is feeling distraught about the state of the college admission situation in our country.

Richard J. Light's *Making the Most of College: Students Speak Their Minds* (Harvard University Press, 2004) though published in 2004, is still incredibly relevant and insightful.

Cal Newport's *How to Become a Straight-A Student: The Unconventional Strategies Real College Students Use to Score High While Studying Less* (Broadway Books, 2007) is a breezy read that has helped many college students develop new tools to succeed academically.

Information on Cost and Aid

The Project on Student Debt (ticas.org/posd/home), run by the Institute for College Access and Success, issued a report on the Class of 2016 that provides a state-by-state analysis of student debt and eye-opening policy recommendations (ticas.org/sites/default/files/pub_files/classof2016.pdf).

U.S. News & World Report assembled a handy table of all schools' Pell-eligible percentages, divided into four categories: national universities, liberal arts colleges, regional universities, and regional colleges. "Economic Diversity: National Universities," *U.S. News & World Report*, colleges.usnews.rankingsandreviews.com/best-colleges/rankings/national-universities/economic-diversity.

FLIP (First-Generation and Low-Income Partnership) is a relatively new organization dedicated to raising awareness of and providing resources for students who are in the first familial generation to go to college. Online at flipnational.org.

Kim Nauer's *FAFSA: The How-To Guide for High School Students and the Adults Who Help Them* is an excellent resource on understanding the first step to getting financial aid at many schools, completing the FAFSA. It is free and downloadable at understandingfafsa.org/assets/FAFSAHowTo201718English.pdf.

In *Paying the Price: College Costs, Financial Aid, and the Betrayal of the American Dream* (University of Chicago Press, 2016), Sara Goldrick-Rab presents the sobering results of her six-year investigation into what she calls "the new economics of college in America."

For eye-opening statistics about "food insecurity" among college students, see the Students Against Hunger site at studentsagainst hunger.org/hunger-on-campus.

On the Transition from High School to College for Students with Disabilities

Navigating the Transition from High School to College for Students with Disabilities, by authors Meg Grigal, Joseph Madaus, Lyman Dukes III, and Debra Hart (Routledge, 2018) helps families navigate the transition from high school to college for students with a wide range of disabilities.

Another resource is *50 Tips for Transitioning from High School to College with a Disability: A Guide for Students Who Have Disabilities and Their Parents,* by R. Michael Schlesinger (author) and Cory Bilicko (editor) (CreateSpace Independent Publishing Platform, 2014).

For Career-Related Reading

NACE, the National Association of Colleges and Employers, has a wealth of information and data that is well researched and illuminating on the best ways for students to prepare for their post-college careers (naceweb.org).

Burning Glass Technologies is an equally impressive organization that aims to "deliver real-time data and breakthrough planning tools that inform careers, define academic programs, and shape work-forces." It is reachable at burning-glass.com.

Designing Your Life: How to Build a Well-Lived, Joyful Life (Alfred A. Knopf, 2016) is Bill Burnett and Dave Evans's Stanford University course turned into a practical guide for everyone on how to use design thinking to build a life at any age.

David Brooks's *The Road to Character* (Random House, 2015) is a fascinating discussion of balancing what he terms "résumé virtues" and "eulogy virtues," helpful for anyone who is contemplating their career.

Ethical Ambition: Living a Life of Meaning and Worth, by Derrick Bell (Bloomsbury Publishing, 2002) offers seven rules for ensuring we put our values at the center of our efforts to construct a successful life.

NOTES

Introduction

xii **The one in three freshmen:** "Freshman Retention Rates: National Universities," *U.S. News & World Report,* colleges.usnews.rankingsandreviews.com/best-colleges/rankings/national-universities/freshmen-least-most-likely-return.

xii **The more than 50 percent:** "Fact Sheet: Focusing Higher Education on Student Success," U.S. Department of Education, July 27, 2017, ed.gov/news/press-releases/fact-sheet-focusing-higher-education-student-success.

xii **Another twenty-eight have graduated:** "What Really Happens to Our Students? Constructing an Estimate of Outcomes for 100 Students Who Start a Bachelor Degree," EAB, October 27, 2017, eab.com/technology/student-success-collaborative/members/infographics/100-students.

xiv **Since the average U.S. high school student:** "Counseling and College Counseling in America's High Schools," National Association of College Admission Counseling (NACAC), January 2005. Since then, the picture has worsened, with national high school enrollment ticking up by 3 percent and the number of counselors increasing by 2 percent (NACAC and American School Counselor Association, *State-by-State Student-to-Counselor Report: 10-Year Trends,* 2015, 6).

Part I

2   **Unless you can pay full freight:** Sara Goldrick-Rab, *Paying the Price: College Costs, Financial Aid, and the Betrayal of the American Dream* (University of Chicago Press, 2016), 1.

Chapter 1

5   **About two-thirds of students:** The Institute for College Access and Success, ticas.org/sites/default/files/pub_files/Debt_Facts _and_Sources.pdf.

6   **About nine of ten first-time:** National Center for Education Statistics, nces.ed.gov/fastfacts/display.asp?id=31.

7   **If a college receives federal funding:** Guidance on Implementing the Net Price Calculator Requirement, Federal Student Aid, February 27, 2013, ifap.ed.gov/dpcletters/GEN1307.html.

11   **"Any student who has difficulty":** Oregon State University's Basic Needs Statement can be found at studentlife.oregonstate .edu/hsrc/other-resources/osu-basic-needs-statement.

23   **Statistics show that:** Project on Student Debt, ticas.org/posd/ home.

23   **Using a student debt calculator:** One example can be found on the Smart Guide to Financial Aid site at finaid.org/calculators/ loanpayments.phtml.

23   **The Hamilton Project:** Diane Whitmore Schanzenbach, Ryan Nunn, and Greg Nantz, "Putting Your Major to Work: Career Paths After College," Brookings Institution, hamiltonproject .org/papers/putting_your_major_to_work_career_paths_after _college.

Chapter 2

37 **"International experience is one"**: Quoted in Ryan Shin, *Convergence of Contemporary Art, Visual Culture, and Global Civic Engagement* (IGI Global, 2017), 119.

38 **"Despite the inevitable increasing global competition"**: Allan Goodman and Stacie Nevadomski Berdan, "Every Student Should Study Abroad," *New York Times,* updated May 12, 2014, nytimes.com/roomfordebate/2013/10/17/should-more -americans-study-abroad/every-student-should-study-abroad.

55 *U.S. News & World Report* **offers a handy table:** "Economic Diversity: National Universities," *U.S. News & World Report,* colleges.usnews.rankingsandreviews.com/best-colleges/rank ings/national-universities/economic-diversity.

58 **In fact, Richard Light:** Richard J. Light, *Making the Most of College: Students Speak Their Minds* (Harvard University Press, 2004), 8.

62 **A number of years ago:** "The Spiritual Life of College Students, a National Study of College Students' Search for Meaning and Purpose," Spirituality in Higher Education, Higher Education Research Institute, Graduate School of Education and Information Studies, University of California, Los Angeles, spirituality .ucla.edu/docs/reports/Spiritual_Life_College_Students_Full _Report.pdf.

71 **Some colleges call them "theme housing":** Wheaton College, "Theme Houses," wheatoncollege.edu/residential-life/housing/ theme-houses.

71 **However, it offers some interesting:** University of Louisville, "Living-Learning and Themed Communities," louisville.edu/ housing/options/llc.

75 **BestColleges.com even publishes:** "Best Dining Halls," best colleges.com/features/best-college-dining-halls.

79 **Harvard's admission office:** "Should I Take Time Off?," Harvard College Admissions and Financial Aid site, college.harvard .edu/admissions/preparing-college/should-i-take-time.

Chapter 3

87 **"Acceptance into all University of California":** Thomas A. Parham, "An Important Message Regarding Fall 2017 Admission," University of California, Irvine, studentaffairs.uci.edu/VC_fall _admissions.php.

97 **In the wake of the globally:** Max Kutner, "The Other Side of the College Sexual Assault Crisis," *Newsweek,* December 10, 2015, newsweek.com/2015/12/18/other-side-sexual-assault-crisis -403285.html.

97 **The theater version of this program:** U.S. Department of Justice, "Protecting Students from Sexual Assault," notalone.gov/ assets/bystander-summary.pdf or justice.gov/ovw/page/file/ 905957/download.

Chapter 4

113 **A recent report by Workday:** Jeffrey J. Selingo, "The Future of Work and What It Means for Higher Education," part 1, "The Changing Workplace and the Dual Threats of Automation and a Gig Economy," Workday, 2, workday.com/content/dam/web/ en-us/documents/reports/future-of-work-part-1.pdf.

114 **"The problem for higher education to solve":** Selingo, "The Future of Work," part 1, 2.

117 **Burning Glass Technologies:** Scott Bittle, "Specific Skills Make Liberal Arts Graduates More Marketable," Burning Glass Technologies, June 9, 2016, burning-glass.com/specific-skills-make -liberal-arts-graduates-more-marketable.

117 **Keeping in mind that:** Selingo, "The Future of Work," 7.

118 **Wellesley College's website:** "The following interactive visualization illustrates the powerful flexibility of a liberal arts degree from Wellesley College," Wellesley College, wellesley.edu/oir/majortocareer.

120 **There are thousands of people:** For an interesting article on students choosing a philosophy major, I recommend this oldie but goodie: Winnie Hu, "In a New Generation of College Students, Many Opt for the Life Examined," *The New York Times*, April 6, 2008, nytimes.com/2008/04/06/education/06philosophy .html.

Chapter 6

187 **But it's interesting to note that:** Marjorie Savage and Chelsea Petree, "National Survey of College and University Parent Programs Survey Conducted Spring 2015," Rochester Institute of Technology, rit.edu/studentaffairs/parentsandfamilies/sites/rit .edu.studentaffairs.parentsandfamilies/files/directory/2015%20 National%20Parent%20Program%20Survey.pdf.

190 **Their "mission is to assist":** College Parents of America, collegeparents.org.

190 **"We believe that parents":** collegeparentcentral.com/about -college-parent-central.

Chapter 7

199 **The institute goes on to state:** National Institute of Alcohol Abuse and Alcoholism, "College Drinking," niaaa.nih.gov/alcohol-health/special-populations-co-occurring-disorders/college-drinking.

200 **A few years ago:** Mosi Secret and Karen Zraick, "5 at Columbia Are Charged in Drug Sales," *New York Times,* December 7, 2010, nytimes.com/2010/12/08/nyregion/08columbia.html.

205 **We are living in an age:** William Deresiewicz, "The Disadvantages of an Elite Education," *The American Scholar,* June 1, 2008, theamericanscholar.org/the-disadvantages-of-an-elite-education.

208 **"Today as never before":** Harold T. Shapiro, *A Larger Sense of Purpose: Higher Education and Society* (Princeton University Press, 2005), 111.

212 **"Passion is not an event":** Derrick Bell, *Ethical Ambition: Living a Life of Meaning and Worth* (Bloomsbury, 2002), 23–24.

212 **"The sacrifice of passion":** Bell, *Ethical Ambition,* 35.

214 **"[Play] is intensely pleasurable":** Stuart Brown with Christopher Vaughan, *Play: How It Shapes the Brain, Opens the Imagination, and Invigorates the Soul* (Penguin, 2009), 4.

INDEX

ABET, 112
academia, careers in, 112, 114
academic departments, 115, 123–24
  community and, 36, 123, 182
  majors and course lists, 115
academic probation, 223
add/drop period, 116–17
  PE and, 67
Adderall, 199, 200
admissions offices, xiv
  application process, 2
  lack of acceptances and, 77–81
  rejections and, 77–78, 83
  revoked, 87–88
  rolling, 77, 83, 88
  senior transcripts and, 86–87
  yield and, 86–89
Admitted Students Days, 2, 62, 66
advisors, 35–36, 39–46, 102, 198. *See also*
    resident advisors
  building community of, 175–86
  evaluations and, 42–43
  first appointment with, 116, 125–26
alcohol and drugs, 59, 61, 80, 148,
    199–201, 213
  awareness training, 97–98
  residential policy on, 160
AlcoholEdu for College, 98
alumni network, 27, 123
Americans with Disabilities Act, 18, 48,
    50, 74
Amherst College, 53, 89–90
anti-racism training, 102
architecture major, 159
athletes. *See also* gym and fitness
    facilities; physical education;
    sports
  disability support and, 49–50
  financial aid and, 21
  varsity, 66–67

athletics fees, 67
attention deficit disorder, 49, 50

bedding, 158–60
Bell, Derrick, 212
Berdan, Stacie Nevadomski, 38
BestColleges.com, 75
bikes, 160
binge-drinking, 199
bipolar disorder, 202
break periods
  cost of, 16
  housing during, 161
  work-study and, 9
Brookings Institution, 23
Brown, Stuart, 214
Burning Glass Technologies, 117
bystander training, 69, 97

campus community, 52–74
  college size and, 27
  cultivating relationships with, 175–85
  dorm life and, 68–74
  Greek organizations and, 59–61
  gym, sports, and PE and, 65–68
  musical options and, 65
  politics and, 63–64
  religion and, 62–63
  sources of support on, 175–85
careers
  advisors and, 121–22, 186
  extracurriculars and, 113
  faculty and, 178
  finding niche and, 208–12
  internships and, 210
  lack of formula for, 110–11
  major and course choices and, 111–23,
    125

careers (*cont.*)
  networking and, 185–87
  parent's, 126–30
  skills needed for, 117–18
career services offices, 120–23, 125
classes. *See* courses
clothing
  what to pack, 157–59
clubs and organizations, 54, 56–58. *See
    also* sports
college acceptances
  lack of, 77–81
  senior transcripts and, 86–87
College Board, 13
college catalog, 112–13
College Confidential, 16, 60, 65
CollegeData.com, 53, 56, 60, 69
college debt, 2, 5–6, 11, 20–21, 23. *See also*
    student loans
College of New Jersey, 70
College Parent Central, 190
College Parents of America, 190
College Scholarship Service (CSS)
    Profile, 13
college town, 26–31
  amenities for parents, 28–29
  cultural opportunities and, 30–31
  demographics and, 26–28
  politics and, 31
  researching, 30–31
  research opportunities and, 27
  size and wealth of, 28–31
  work opportunities and, 30–31
Columbia University, 56–57, 70, 97
Common Application, 86
communication plan, 146–49, 163
  medical needs and, 149, 202
community service, 28
computers, 159
cost of attendance, xiv, 2, 5–24
  books and, 7, 16
  breaks and, 16
  calculating net, 7
  course fees and, 7
  extracurricular activities and, 7, 16
  food and housing insecurity and, 11
  Greek life and club fees, 59–60
  health insurance and, 17–19
  housing and, 69
  laundry and, 7
  pre-orientation and, 100
  "sticker price," 7, 13

  student health services and, 155
  transportation and, 7
  work-study, and 8–10
courses/classes, xv
  add/drop period and, 116–17
  choosing before registration, 109–16,
    125–26
  class participation and attendance,
    221
  class size and, 34–36
  college "fit" and, 32–33
  overloading, 135–36
  registration and, 93, 102
  syllabus for, and grades, 220–21
  time management and, 131–38
  types of professors or grad students
    teaching, 34–36
credit hours
  full-time status and, 126
  PE classes and, 66
  study hours and, 51, 132–34, 138
cross-registration options, 32
culture shock, 171–75
  adjustment phase, 173–74
  diversity and, 197–99
  honeymoon phase, 172–73
  independence phase, 174–75
  withdrawal phase, 173

decision-making period, xiii, xiv, 1–2
  academic advising list for, 41–42
  financial considerations, 5–25
  fit considerations, 26–81
  health and disability support and,
    47–52
  pre-deposit list, 52
  research list for, 30–31
DePauw University, 60
depression, 148–49
Deresiewicz, William, 205
dining halls, 16, 47, 75–76. *See also* food
disabilities, 47–52
  dorm assignments and, 95–96
  forms for, 92
  PE and, 68
diversity, 53–54, 196–99
  training and, 97
dormitories, 68–74. *See also* resident
    advisors
  activities in, 69, 73
  amenities and, 74

bedding and, 158–60
breaks and, 16, 161
capacities of, 86–87, 96
cooking and, 75–76, 160
furnishings for, 156, 160–61
housing form and, 93–96
insurance and, 161
laundry and, 160
living-learning or theme communities
    and, 71–73
maintenance staff and, 176
off-campus housing vs., 69
orientation and, 102–3
packing and, 156–57
policy manual for, 160–61
reassignment requests and, 74
residential advisors and, 71–72
roommates and, 70
rule violations and, 161
sending packages to, 159
summer housing and, 161
support structure in, 74, 95, 176
dropouts, xii

eating clubs, 60
effective altruism, 211
electronics, 159, 205–7
emergencies, 10, 153
Emory College, 189
empty-nest feeling, 128
engineering majors, 112, 114, 159
Estimated Family Contribution (EFC),
    10–11, 14
Ethical Ambition (Bell), 212
Excellent Sheep (Deresiewicz), 205
extracurricular activities, 80, 112
    career and, 119
    choosing, 113, 117–18
    clubs and, 56–58
    costs and, 7, 16
    orientation and, 101–2
    time management and, 132–35, 138

Facebook, 16, 61, 95
faculty, xiii
    academic fit and, 33–37
    class size and, 34
    cultivating relationships with, 36, 52,
        175–86, 222–23
    deadlines and extensions and, 220

dinners and activities with, 72
emailing, 179–80
fall semester and, 87
full-time tenured, vs. adjuncts and grad
    students, 34–35
grade disputes and, 220–22
letters of recommendation and, 178
office hours and, 35–36, 177, 179, 219,
    222
parent and, 190–91, 221–22
politics and, 63
residence halls and, 72
size of, 53
student evaluations of, 36
-student ratio, 33–37
study abroad and, 39
webpages and CV of, 179
FAFSA, 6, 13
fall schedule, 131–38
    end of semester plan and, 219
    exercise to prepare, 133–34
    extracurriculars and, 131–33, 138
    leisure time and, 133, 137
    overloading, 135–36
    preparing realistic, xv, 109–26
    required courses and, 136–37
    sleep and dining time, 133
    strategies for creating, 137–38
    study time and, 132–33
Family Educational Rights and Privacy
    Act (FERPA, 1974), 152–53
    release form, 153
finals, 9, 132, 213, 219
financial aid, 6
    annual tuition increases and, 20
    appealing award, 12–13
    applying every year, 14
    applying late, 14
    athletes and, 21
    breaks and, 16
    cap on semesters and, 20
    change in circumstances and, 13–14
    comfort level and, 22–23
    cost gap and, 10, 14
    course and activities fees and, 16
    EFC and, 10–11, 14
    GPA and, 21
    health insurance and, 17–19
    orientation and, 102
    outside sources of, 14–15
    self-help and, 11
    senior transcript and, 88

financial aid (*cont.*)
  student leaves and, 21
  study abroad and, 12, 15
  summer earnings and, 21–22
  tuition grants, 10
  work-study and, 8–10
financial aid officer, 12–13
first-generation students, 53, 55, 198
fit, 2, 26–81
FLIP (First-Generation Low-Income
    Partnership), 55
food, 172
  cooking options, 75–76, 160
  costs of, 7, 11, 16
  dining halls and, 75–76
  dorm refrigerator and, 94, 160
  return home and, 227
food allergies, 75
food and housing insecurity, 11
foreign language classes, 39, 50
Foreign Service, 119
formula-for-life problem, 109–14
fraternities, 58–61
free time, 131–38
freshman seminars, 34, 209
friendships, 213
  high school, 91, 92, 144–46, 197–98,
    213
  parent's new networks of, 224–26
  student's new network of, 224–28
fundraising, 6, 187–88

gap year, 78–81, 88
gender-based training, 97
Gettysburg College, 191–92
Goldman Sachs, 111
Goldrick-Rab, Sara, 2
goodbyes, 144–46, 163–64, 166–67
Goodman, Allan E., 37–38
grades and GPA, 218–23
  academic probation and, 223
  disputes or appeals over, 220–22
  financial aid and, 21
  less than hoped for, 220–23
  policies, rubrics, and guidelines on,
    220–21, 223
  sharing with parent, 153
  study abroad and, 39
  study time and deadlines and, 218–20
graduate schools, 32–33
graduate students, 34–35, 72, 180
graduation rate, 14

Greek life, 58–61
Grinnell College, 63
gym and fitness facilities, 48, 65. *See
    also* athletes; physical education;
    sports

Hagerty, Barbara Bradley, 169
Hamilton Project, 23
Hampshire College, 53
Harvard University, 79, 90, 119–20
  Law School, 180
hazing, 59
health care, 17–19, 149–55. *See also*
    disabilities; psychological needs;
    student health services
health insurance, 17–19
  club sports and, 67
  college insurance policy, 155
  family waiver and, 155
high school
  dangers of senior slump, 85–90
  friends and, 144–45, 197–98, 213
  guidance counselor and, xiv, 40
  senior transcripts and, 86–89
Hillel, 57
HIPPA privacy rule, 152, 154
holidays, 173, 185, 213, 227–28
homesickness, 173–75
housing. *See also* dormitories
  application form, 92, 93–96
  costs of, 11, 16
  on- vs. off-campus, 69
Human Services Resource Center
    (HRSC), 11

Individuals with Disabilities Education
    Act (IDEA), 50
informational interviewing, 129–30
Institute for International Education, 37
institutes and centers, 32–33, 115
International SOS, 18
internships, 27–28, 32–33, 117, 133–34,
    187, 210

jobs, 28, 33. *See also* careers; internships;
    work-study
  career service office and, 120–23
  college location and, 30–31
  college size and, 27–28
  connections and, 185–86

extracurriculars and, 117, 119
gap year and, 79–80
GPA and, 223
off-campus, 10–11
summer, 10–11, 21–22

Kalamazoo College, 71
Kennedy, Caroline, 1
Kenyon College, 29, 64

Latino or Hispanic students, 54
laundry, 160, 227
law school, 111, 119, 126
learning disabilities, 48–50
leisure time, 7, 27–28, 30–31, 133
LGBTQA issues, 48, 55, 71, 198
    training and, 97
Life Reimagined (Hagerty), 169
Light, Richard, 58
living-learning communities, 71
loneliness, 138. *See also* homesickness;
    solitude, practice of
love relationships, 224–26

Macalester College, 30, 189
majors, 32, 34–35, 109, 111, 114–26, 178
    advisors and, 42
    anxiety about, 125
    careers and, 117–20
    course selection and, 115–18
    grades and, 221
    independent, 123–26
    learning about, 114–20, 123
    number of undergrads in, 35
    requirements and, 42, 136–37
mathematics majors, 112, 114
medical school, 111, 119, 126, 209
midterms, 132, 213
mind-body classes, 47
mindfulness, 205–7
minors, 32, 34, 111, 115–16, 123, 136
MIT, 151–52
Model UN, 119
Mount Holyoke College, 53
move-in, xv
    packing for, 156–59
    schedule, 102
    summer job before, 22
musical opportunities, for non–music
    majors, 65

National Association of Colleges and
    Employers (NACE), 117, 119
National Institute on Alcohol Abuse and
    Alcoholism, 199

Oberlin College, 29, 64
off-campus housing, 70
office hours, 177, 179, 219
Operation Ivy League, 200
Oregon State University, 11
orientation, 97, 146–48

packages, sending, 159
packing, 156–59, 163
Parent and Family Office, 93, 188–91
parent councils, 188
Parents' Weekend, 159
Parham, Thomas A., 87
partying, 199–203
peer advisors, 42, 43
peer education programs, 48
peer health advocates, 204
Pell Grants, 55
pets, 160
philosophy major, 119–20
physical disabilities, 48, 68
physical education (PE), 65–68. *See also*
    athletes; gym and fitness facilities;
    sports
    disability exemptions, 68
    fees and, 67
    medical certification and, 68
    registration and deadlines, 67
play, 214–17
political dynamics, 63–64, 196, 198
pre–culture shock, 90–92
pre-orientation, 98–101
prescription drugs, 149, 151, 155, 201–3
    abuse of, 199–201
Princeton University, 60–61, 79
Project on Student Debt, 11, 21
psychological needs
    communication plan and, 148–49
    informing college about, 150–52, 154–55
    medication and, 201–3
    support for, 47–49

Reed College, 64
registration
    advising meeting before, 126

registration (*cont.*)
  choosing courses and, 109–16, 125
  orientation and, 102
  PE classes and, 66–67
  summer, 113
religion and spirituality
  diversity and, 197–98
  parent and, 107
  student and, 31, 62–63, 71, 196, 207
Religious Life Office, 62
requirements, 133, 136
  distribution or core, 136
  freshman, 126
  majors and, 42, 136–37
  PE, 66, 68
research opportunities, 28, 32–33, 178,
  182
residences. *See* dormitories; roommates
resident advisors (RAs) 69, 70–71, 94–95,
  102, 151, 191, 198, 202
residential life office, 71
résumés, 117, 119
roommates, 70, 74, 172–73
  housing form and, 93–96
  orientation and, 102–3
  reassignments and, 74, 94–96
Rotary Club scholarships, 14
ROTC students, 66, 71
Rutgers University, 70, 97

salary, post-college
  average by major, 23
  monthly loan payments and, 23–24
Sallie Mae, 12
scholarships, outside, 14–15
science majors, 112, 114
SCREAM (Students Challenging Realities
  and Educating Against Myths), 97
self-guidedness, 183–84
seminar courses, 178
serendipity time, 137–38
service learning, 28
sex, 80, 203–4, 213, 226
sexual assault, 97, 204
  prevention training, 97, 147
sexual harassment training, 97, 102
sexual health promotion, 48
Shapiro, Harold, 208
Shin, Elizabeth, 151–54
Siena College, 33
sleep and rest, 91–92, 133–34, 161–63,
  213, 226–27

Smith College, 53
smoking, 47, 160
social activism, 64, 71, 196, 207–13
social life. *See also* campus community
  clubs and organizations and, 54, 56–58
  diversity and, 196–99
  dorms and, 68–74
  finding niche and, 207–12
  Greek life and, 58–61
  partying and, 199–203
  political dynamics and, 63–64
  practicing solitude and, 204–7
  sex and, 203–4
  sports and PE classes, 65–68
  time management and, 133
Social Security, 12
socioeconomic diversity, 54–55, 198
sociology majors, 118–19
solitude, practice of, 205–7
sororities, 58–61
special-interest students, 188
Spirituality in Higher Education Research
  Group, 62
sports, 65–68, 91. *See also* athletes; gym
  and fitness facilities; physical
  education
  club or intramural, 48, 65, 67, 92
state vs. private colleges, costs and, 24
Stony Brook University, 78
Student Affairs or Success Office, 189,
  199
student body
  geographic diversity of, 28, 53
  Greek organization percentages and,
  59–60
  politics and, 63–64
  size of, 53
  socioeconomic diversity of, 54–55
student fees, 58, 67
student health services, 47–51, 149–55.
  See also disabilities; health care; health
  insurance; psychological needs
student loans
  calculating total debt, 20–21, 23
  deferment option, 5
  EFC-grants gap and, 10–11
  financial aid package and, 20–21
  interest rates on, 5–6
  monthly payments and, 23–24
  reading loan agreements, 6
  repayment start dates, 5–6
Student Organizations, Office of, 57
student union, 66

study abroad, 112
  financial aid and, 12, 15
  health insurance and, 18–19
  opportunities for, 37–39, 52
study and homework time
  deadlines and extensions and, 220
  end of first semester and, 218–20
  requirements per class hour, 132–34,
    138
suicide attempts, 151–52
summer before move-in, 83–84, 109–68
  choosing courses and majors during,
    109–26
  choosing extracurriculars during, 113,
    138
  choosing fall schedule during, 109–23,
    130–38, 138
  packing and, 149–61, 163
  parent and, 126–30, 138–43
  pre-orientation and, 100–101
  preparing goodbyes and, 144–46,
    163–66
  rest and, 161–63
  setting up health networks during,
    149–56, 163
summer family vacation, 100–101
summer housing and storage, 161
summer programs
  mandatory, 96–98, 102
  pre-orientation, 98–101
  scholarships to cover earnings
    requirements, 21–22

Teach for America (TFA), 209–10
televisions, 158
Thanksgiving, 173, 185, 213
theme housing, 71
time management, 131–38, 205–7
toiletries, 158–59
town-gown tensions, 31
transcript, 113
  deadlines and extensions and, 220

dropped and incomplete classes, 67, 220
experiential, 113
PE classes and, 67
transportation and travel, 30
  costs and, 7, 16
  study abroad and, 15
Trinity College, 33
Tufts University, 44
tutors, 50

University Life, Office of, 97
University of California, Irvine, 87–88
University of Indianapolis, 60–61
University of Louisville, 71
University of Massachusetts, Amherst, 53
University of North Carolina, Chapel Hill,
  24, 57
University of Vermont, 64
U.S. News & World Report, 55, 59, 60

Virginia Tech shootings, 152
volunteer work, 27, 112

Wellesley College, 118
wellness initiatives, 47–49, 151
Wheaton College, 71
winter break, xvi
Workday, 113
work-study
  break periods, 9
  finals and, 9
  finances and, 8–10
  flexibility of, 9
  job options and, 33
  relationships with adults at, 182
  time management and, 133–34
  travel costs and time, 9

yield, 86–88

ABOUT THE AUTHOR

MONIQUE RINERE, a first-generation college student, earned a B.A. from Hunter College, and an M.A. and a Ph.D. from Princeton University. She was a residential college dean at Princeton, founded the Advising Programs Office at Harvard University, and served as the dean of advising for Columbia University. As associate vice president for student success, she now leads academic advising, career development, academic integrity, and student health services, among other student-centered initiatives, at the New School. Monique is also a therapist at the Theodor Reik Clinical Center for Psychotherapy and lives in New York City with her husband, Benedict Gedaminski, and their dog, Toby.

moniquerinere.com

ABOUT THE TYPE

This book was set in Minion, a 1990 Adobe Originals typeface by Robert Slimbach (b. 1956). Minion is inspired by classical, old-style typefaces of the late Renaissance, a period of elegant, beautiful, and highly readable type designs. Created primarily for text setting, Minion combines the aesthetic and functional qualities that make text type highly readable with the versatility of digital technology.